Across Dusk to Dawn

Sharifah Nadirah

Published by:

Unit No. E-10-5, Jalan SS15/4G, Subang Square,
47500 Subang Jaya, Selangor.
+603-5612-2407
info@tertib.press
www.tertib.press
@tertibpress (Facebook & Instagram)

Author	:	Sharifah Nadirah
Editor	:	Norashikin Azizan
Cover designer	:	Faris Akmal Faizal
Typesetter	:	Inda Hayati Samsi

ACROSS DUSK TO DAWN

First Edition: May 2024

Perpustakaan Negara Malaysia

Cataloguing-in-Publication Data

A catalogue record for this book is available from the National Library of Malaysia

ISBN: 978-967-2844-36-5

Copyright © Sharifah Nadirah 2024

All rights reserved.
No part of this publication may be reproduced, distributed, or transmitted in any form or by any means, including photocopying, recording, or other electronic or mechanical methods, without the prior written permission of Tertib Publishing.
Printed in Malaysia.

CONTENTS

Foreword   5

On Hope

Meeting Your Inner Child   12
Eliminating Toxicity   51
Across Dusk to Dawn   81

On Love

The Passionate Muslim   128
Knowing Thyself   151
Facing Discrimination   173
Facing Judgemental People   185

On Contentment

Taking Care of Mental Health	193
Embracing Self-healing	213
Failure, Challenges, Hope and Success	228

Glossary	248
References	251

FOREWORD

In *Across Dusk to Dawn*, we embark on a journey through the twilight of uncertainty into the radiant dawn of hope, love and contentment. Sharifah Nadirah invites us to explore the intricacies of life's transitions, the beauty of resilience, and the profound lessons hidden in the fibre of everyday experiences through her personal narratives.

As pages turn, we are reminded again and again to cherish every moment in our lives—good and bad—because the fleeting nature of time will make us desperately long for our 'inner child' that might exist only in the past.

Serving as a beacon of hope and solace, *Across Dawn to Dusk* guides us through the darkness of doubt and despair towards the light of faith and perseverance.

Through her vivid storytelling and heartfelt reflections, the author encourages us to embrace change, to seek knowledge in the face of ignorance, and to find strength in our vulnerabilities. *Across Dusk to Dawn* is not just a book; it is a testament to the soul's ability to triumph over adversity and emerge stronger and wiser—just like a phoenix who rises from the ashes.

May *Across Dusk to Dawn* illuminate your path in the dusk, bring you to the dawn and inspire you to embrace each new day with courage and optimism.

Tertib Publishing

To the hearts who are in need of comfort in a friend,

may these words be your warm companion across the darkest nights,

throughout your journey in embracing light.

On Hope

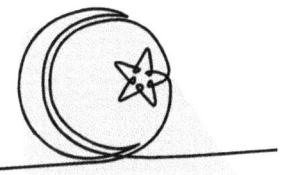

Her chest felt unease and tight

She felt fearful in facing the fight

But she fought with all her soulful might

She stand strong in the darkest night

She hold firm to God's guide

She believed she would be alright

Under the radiating brilliance of moonlight

She was a seeker of His merciful light

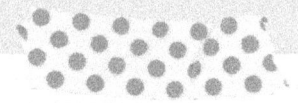

Dear inner child,

It's been a while since we last met. Can you still remember the glorious days of our carefree souls? Can you still remember how unbothered we were? We were once genuinely happy. We were driven to joy and laughter. We breathe in hope and hold on to live happily ever after. We believe in magic and have mythical creatures from our bedtime stories as our heroes, and find fairy tales as our childhood inspiration. We have faith in the beauty of the world, and we seek daily miracles. Our minds aspire us to reach beyond infinity, while our hearts are tuned to the melodies of love and endless possibilities. We were in high spirits to rule the world and become the masterminds. There was not much to think about except running here and there without needing to know our whereabouts. Our imaginations roared louder than thunder and our courage was like no other. At that very moment, we were alive and for once, we felt real. As we make way for adulthood, in a blink of an eye everything that was so dear to us disappeared in thin air.

All of a sudden we feel strange—living in a world that is bound to please rather than having our own soul at ease. We worry endlessly about everything. We get stressed out on what people say about us. We feel afraid of how people might view us. We don't want to be judged and looked down on. We would always work on meeting the unhealthy expectations of others even though it hurts us and no longer makes us feel true to ourselves. We will always have to participate in any rat race and compete to see who is much more worthy. Adulthood is indeed mentally challenging. All we ever want as an adult is to feel enough, to be seen, heard, validated, supported, celebrated, appreciated and belonged, but somehow those are the things we struggled to gain day and night in this grown-up journey of ours. We often feel tired and exhausted from having to deal with everything while nobody understands us and we feel that the world is against us. Everything appears so messy and overwhelming. And we would see emotionally troubled adults around us who have mostly disconnected from their inner child. What we commonly see are only soulless bodies wandering and lost.

I am afraid that I will join them too soon. I am worried about losing you and I do hope I will be given the strength and wisdom to keep on pursuing you and having you as a blessing in life.

Yours truly,

The Adult Version of You

MEETING YOUR INNER CHILD

Yearning to be a child

Isn't it ironic how we yearn to grow up fast during our childhood days but then now once we are an adult we want to become a kid again? Now when we are bigger in size, we often picture the little version of us running excitedly at the playground and doing silly dances in the middle of the crowd shamelessly. The imagination made us feel how carefree it would be to be a child again—not worrying about what people would think of us, not having heavy stuff to think about and complicated things to face. But then there was the child version of us who had dreamed of growing up fast. That little version of us who believed that the grown-up world was filled with freedom and joy. That little kid who would always hope that she could taste the joy of adulthood overnight. That little girl who had a dream of wanting to wear make-up, grown-up clothes and having an adult version handbag of her own.

It was very desirable to grow into an adult when I witnessed how powerful the adults appear. It is as if they could do anything and everything they want without curfews and restrictions. They were free and in control of their life. And that little version of me was eager to join "them". My childhood dream of becoming an adult besides having adult attire is to visit all the theme parks and toy stores around the world and watching my favourite cartoon show from day to night without being told to go to bed. I couldn't wait to have my own job, money, house and car. I wanted to be free. I was pumped and thrilled to grow up when I was little. That was before I grew up to be an adult and realised that things were not really the same as I had imagined. All this while I believed that the adult world was all I needed to break free.

The truth is being a "grown-up" seems so exciting when we're young, especially when we are asked by grown-ups what we want to be when we grow up. Such a question allows us to picture an abundance of imagination in that little head of ours, but it gives you a different unexpected picture when you have reached adulthood. What we were never aware of is that being an adult is challenging; we also need to struggle to be in balance of nearly everything. There are a lot of things that need to be attentive, focused and concerned about. You have to make sure that everything gets done, and you have to be fully accountable for your actions and words. You have to pay bills, monitor your bank accounts, get up on time, eat healthily, effectively manage your time, mind your words, mind your manners and the list goes on. Apparently, things are not that simple like how I thought it would be. When I was a child, I looked around at other adults and assumed they were all perfect and everything in their lives were falling into place. I thought everyone appeared to be in tune.

However, that turns out not to be true. As an adult myself now, I realise that we all have our own emotional struggles and battles and that nobody has it together. All of us are trying our best to make it through the day, to survive and live life. Never have I thought in those childhood days that adulthood can also be incredibly and adventurously challenging. There are so many journeys in life—soul-searching, life meaning, purpose finding, true calling, career-exploration, self-love path, self-discovery, healing road and growth journeys—they all demanded to be embarked on. While the collection of journeys has taught us progress and growth, our inner balance will be tested throughout those journeys. We will also be tested with restlessness, confusion, anxiety, loss, depression and feeling stuck along the way and we all might also experience mental health problems at one point in life. It is stated in the Qur'an:

"We will surely test you with something of fear, hunger, loss of wealth, lives, and fruits, but give glad tidings to the patient, who went disaster strikes them, say 'Indeed, we belong to Allah, and indeed to Him we will return.'" (saheeh international)

(*surah* al-Baqarah, 2:155–56)

It is Allah's (s.w.t.) promise that He will place mankind in hardships, calamities, tribulations, troubles, problems and trials of different kinds, all of which will bring a natural response of anxiety in us. We are bound to be afflicted by hardships even if we are about to run from it or whether we respond to it in a positive or negative way. Some people despise the world because they have experienced a great deal of hardship, stress, and exhaustion in it. But we can't blame people for not understanding the true nature of the world as a place of trials because even those who have understood it are still struggling daily to face such reality where this world is a place for us to succeed. The truth is in His wisdom, Allah (s.w.t.)

tests us with difficulties so we can learn about ourselves—our inner selves including our heart, our mind, our soul, our emotions, our spirit, our personalities, our mental state and our inner child—all of these for us to recognise our truest self. This is similar to an alchemist who melts gold and silver to remove its impurities; Allah (s.w.t.) likewise puts us to trial in order to remove our impure spiritual qualities and allow only our best pure qualities remain.

Thus, hardships can bring out the best in people, just as they can bring out the worst in people. If we deeply contemplate all the experiences of facing hardship, we will realise that we would usually grow stronger from the difficulties. And this is the nature of trials; they are opportunities and ways for growth. But it is understood that the mere experience of dealing with hardships is indeed testing. In our journey to accept life's hardships, we occasionally find ourselves longing to return to simpler times, escaping momentarily from reality. We wanted to be the little version of ourselves again. Imagining the little version of us who was free-spirited, innocent, pure-hearted, playful and joyful made me want to teleport to the past. I would start to miss the little version of myself who was an explorer, a young adventurer who sets out on fresh expeditions through fantastical realms of imagination. The child who often gets lost in her playtime, making endless visits to playgrounds, toy stores and ice cream vendors while radiating genuine warm smiles and laughter. It is my desire to reconnect with her. She holds everything that I want to reclaim. I aspire to pursue that little girl who was free-spirited, courageous, believing, hopeful, faithful, cheerful and playful.

Why was I not grateful back then and why am I not seeking the current moments of beauty? Sigh.

Indeed, mankind is always in a state of dissatisfaction, ungratefulness and this reminds me of a verse in the Qur'an:

> *"And He gave you from all you asked of Him. And if you should count the favour [i.e., blessings] of Allah, you could not enumerate them. Indeed, mankind is [generally] most unjust and ungrateful."*
>
> (*surah* Ibrahim, 14:34)

This really hits me hard. Indeed, by practising contentment and gratitude, it could contribute to our inner balance and peace. I learned that I should have been thankful of where I was, where I am and where I shall be, because our Lord is indeed Wise and Most Compassionate. There is indeed hidden wisdom for where we are placed in life and for where we are in every phase of our lives starting from the day we are born up until now. There is a reason why we are all placed in a process of growth and now that I understand that, it somehow did make me feel guilty. I also regretted wanting to be an adult so badly in those childhood days of mine. Nowadays when the thought of being a child is much more intriguing, I learn to embrace such nostalgic memories and gradually work on being content with what I am and what I have at the moment.

The Prophet (s.a.w.) and emotional trauma

We live in a world where there are many emotionally troubled adults wandering around in circles to find a way out of their trauma. Emotional trauma has a unique way of throwing us off balance. It holds you back from living life at its fullest. It stops you from discovering love and distancing you from your true self. It halts you from growth and blows out your light of hopefulness. People are bound to run into all sorts of difficulties in life, including traumatising events. Childhood trauma can have an enduring impact on a person's soul and psyche and us Muslims are not free from these kinds of hardships either. It is important for us to recognise the trauma we have, regardless of culture or religion, because traumatising events are real, and it is a part of the human experience. It's important for us to realise that being Muslim does not shield us from hardship or suffering. But instead, Allah (s.w.t.) says in the Qur'an:

> *"Do the people think that they will be left to say, 'We believe' and they will not be tried? But We have certainly tried those before them, and Allah (s.w.t.) will surely make evident those who are truthful, and He will surely make evident the liars."*
>
> (*surah* al-'Ankabut, 29:2-3)

What I personally reflected on the *surah* was that Allah (s.w.t.) put us through tests, trials and tribulations to see if we would still willingly follow and obey His commands or reject His teaching. This reminds me of Prophet Muhammad (s.a.w.) who had experienced numerous hardships and challenges in his lifetime that shaped his mental, emotional, and spiritual strength. His experiences shaped the character of the man who carried the weight of the revelation and was responsible for spreading the message of Islam, allowing him to persevere through every calamity. Thus, everyone is not immune towards such challenges given in life and no human is immune towards emotional troubles. Even Prophet Muhammad (s.a.w.)

experienced intense grief and sorrow. There was a moment when Prophet Muhammad (s.a.w.) experienced a decline in his health as he was affected by concern for those who opposed Islam in Makkah and so, Allah (s.w.t.) revealed the *ayah*:

> *Then perhaps you would kill yourself through grief over them, [O' Muḥammad], if they do not believe in this message, [and] out of sorrow.*
>
> (*surah* al-Kahf, 18:6)

Thus, we can learn from his life that going through emotional pain is a part of being human. When a person is facing emotional pain and bearing the weight of one's trauma, it is not a sign of a lack of *iman* or self-awareness on the part of Muslims. But instead, in actuality, admitting our pain, suffering and asking for help reveals our humanity and bravery. Prophet Muhammad (s.a.w.) was always ready to help people through their trauma towards hope and relief. The Prophet never associated sadness with a lack of faith. Rather than dismissing people's experiences and emotions, he acknowledged them, reassured them, and helped them in gaining perspective and hope. People often came to the Prophet (s.a.w.) to share their grief, knowing they would be taken seriously, listened to, and respected. The Prophet (s.a.w.) offered empathy and support, as well as prayers to help them move forward. Hence showing that in these times of need, asking for help, relying on one another for support, and turning to Allah (s.w.t.) are acts of bravery and devotion that shows how our faith embraces every aspect of our lives, including our challenges and our healing journey.

The Holistic Approach to Heal

The Islamic faith provides a framework for understanding and overcoming this emotional pain and traumatic events, reassuring us that Allah (s.w.t.) is our source of strength and that we are never alone on our journey of healing. In difficult times, we are told to turn to Allah (s.w.t.) and remember that He is with us so we can find ease in prayer, make *duʿaʾ* and see it as a powerful tool that Allah (s.w.t.) is giving the believer, engaging in *dhikr* which is a great way to remind ourselves that Allah (s.w.t.) is here with us and draw strength from the Qur'an's wisdom. It is mentioned in the Qur'an that:

> *"And your Lord says, "Call upon Me; I will respond to you…"*
>
> (*surah* Ghafir, 40:60)

This serves as a reminder that Allah (s.w.t.) is the greatest comforter and source of strength for everyone who is in need. Allah (s.w.t.) had promised that if we call upon Him, He will indeed respond. It is for sure and without doubt Allah (s.w.t.) hears us as He is 'The Responsive', 'The Answerer' and 'The Acceptor of Invocation'. He is here for us to call upon Him at all times, including in times of joy, disappointment or contentment and especially in times of need. However, it's important to understand that from an Islamic perspective, healing is a holistic approach that incorporates one's physical, emotional, and spiritual needs. The Islamic teaching emphasises the importance of both evidence-based therapy and spiritual healing, encouraging a balance between turning to Allah (s.w.t.) and getting professional help. It doesn't matter if we choose to seek professional assistance or turn to Allah (s.w.t.); in many situations, we should do both. This is consistent with Islamic teachings, which promote action and the pursuit of solutions to our problems. Thus, while asking Allah (s.w.t.) for guidance and help is very important, it's also critical to take proactive measures for healing and progress, including getting professional help when required.

Self-healing Approach

A holistic approach suggested by the Islamic teaching is in alignment with the current science evidence-based. Susan Trachman, M.D, who is an associate professor at George Washington University and is a board-certified psychiatrist stated that:

"Holistic psychiatry is an emerging approach to mental healthcare that emphasises the underlying biological, psychological, and social factors contributing to mental health issues. It considers the unique genetic, environmental, and lifestyle factors influencing each individual's mental health."

Thus from such a holistic approach we are able to then understand each individual's traumatic events and unique responses.

Furthermore, during my years of therapy, my psychologist told me that within the umbrella of the adopted holistic approach, there exists the self-healing method. The self-healing method is crucial to be incorporated into the holistic approach in one's recovery journey. The self-healing is about taking responsibility for our well-being and actively working towards our own healing. Self-healing doesn't necessarily mean that we should dismiss modern medicine, doctors, psychologists, psychiatrists, counsellors, and also to no longer seek the right support and resources that can aid us in our journey and completely rely on ourselves to heal; it's an additional way suggested by therapist in aiding this recovery journey of ours. I find the self-healing method is a tailor-made healing approach which is absolutely intriguing as it gives us the freedom to pave our own personal healing journey by doing the things we love. When it comes to a personal healing journey of oneself, there is indeed no fixed solution for everyone.

Everyone has their own way of being in a perfect balance and in control again. We all have our unique way to be awakened and guided towards recovery. The self-healing method includes incorporating activities of your likings. Some people find solace in watching the sunset or find peace while walking along the beach, while others might indulge in creative activities such as writing, painting, or reading. Reading has become a form of self-healing therapy for me, particularly when I delve into books focused on healing themes related to the inner child. These books not only resonate with me but also serve as a therapeutic method, aiding in my recovery. Besides working on reconnecting with my inner child with the help of my psychologist, I was also advised by my psychologist on finding personal ways to reconnect with that inner child of mine via reading, understanding and practice. Hence, here I would like to share my personal way of adopting the self-healing method in the following subchapter which might also resonate with others.

The Inner Child, **A Poetic Metaphor**

Do you remember when I mentioned how as adults, we sometimes wish we could be kids again? It seems impossible, and even just becoming childlike again is difficult because we're all so preoccupied with our busy lives. I just wanted to tell you that, it is not that impossible for you to be a child again, you can be one once again and this is where the concept of reconnecting with our inner child comes. We all have an 'inner child', whether we realise it or not. When it comes to the inner child, it is not only a poetic metaphor to talk about. It's speaking of a mental model—a subconscious holdover from our past selves as kids that frequently affects our emotions, behaviours, and reactions. In psychotherapy, the phrase 'Inner Child' has been used for what seems like ages. The inner child is commonly associated with your early childhood self, and it represents your personality's purity, authenticity, and vulnerability. Your inner child is the most authentic expression of your emotions, creativity, and wonder. It's the part of you that finds joy in the simple things, welcomes playfulness and has an open mind about the world. It is stated in the book titled *The Recovery of Your Inner Child: The Highly Acclaimed Method for Liberating Your Inner Self* by Lucia Capphacione, Ph.D. that:

> *"The Inner Child lives within all of us, it's the part of us that feels emotions and is playful, intuitive, and creative. Usually hidden under our grown-up personas, the Inner Child holds the key to intimacy in relationships, physical and emotional well-being, recovery from addictions, and the creativity and wisdom of our inner selves"*

Within each adult, there exists a 'little version' or inner child. However, the demands and pressures of adult life often cover up this joyful and innocent aspect of ourselves with layers of negative emotions such as doubts, confusion, anger, frustration, disappointment, and worry. Life can be hectic and demanding, and in the midst of adulthood, we may lose touch with our inner child which is a significant part of ourselves. The truth is it is indeed too easy to lose touch with our inner child's carefree and imaginative spirit in this chaotic life.

Losing our inner child

As we grow older, we somehow feel distant from our inner child. We start to lose sight of the little things that made us grateful, the childish things that make us smile, giggle and laugh. We start judging one's inclination towards childish stuff, such as watching cartoons or eating childish meals or food. We misinterpret one's inner child for immaturity and we start to create more space between the adult version of ourselves and our inner child. The distance and space we created had separated us from genuineness and allowed our ego, societal expectations, greed, and other negative qualities to halt our journey to progress. Most of us had lost our inner child along the journey and each and one of us are continuously searching for the meaning and purpose of our life. Along the road, we encounter obstacles and hardships, and sometimes we might feel disoriented and unsure.

This reminds me of a verse in the Qur'an.

"And He found you lost and guided [you],"

(*surah* aḍ-Ḍuḥa, 93:7)

It is a profound *ayah* that reminds us of how merciful and compassionate Allah (s.w.t.) is towards His creations. It is a verse that resonates with the hearts of the believers in reminding us that we were once lost, but through His guidance, we have found our way, in His infinite mercy and grace, He led us down the right path. This guidance is not limited to our spiritual journey; it applies to all parts of our lives. Hence it inspires those who feel lost—those who had lost their inner child, to be hopeful again as it shows that we humans would tend to get lost throughout this long journey of ours. We will all at one point lose that inner child of ours and want to re-seek it. It is indeed a part and parcel of life.

And when it comes to understanding the 'lost' inner child, it is said to be a psychological and personal development concept that refers to a part of your emotional and psychological self that has become disconnected, neglected, or wounded over time. When the inner child is described as 'lost,' it usually means that this part of your psyche has been suppressed, ignored, or pushed aside by life experiences, trauma, societal expectations, or personal coping mechanisms. When we grow up, we tend to lose the childishness and cheerfulness in us and become disconnected from our inner child. The overly demanding modern life that throws us in a loop of never-ending workload such as managing household, job, finances, and other stressors, can overwhelm our inner child. The stress and anxiety that originated from such commitments can reduce our ability to enjoy life's simple pleasures and embrace spontaneity. The responsibilities and demands of everyday life can take up a lot of your time as you enter adulthood. The practicalities of adult life may overshadow the sense of wonder and spontaneity that characterised our early years.

We forget our inner child's goals and aspirations. We rarely choose to be ourselves anymore in fear of being rejected and engage in self-criticism, perfectionism, and self-judgement. Our ability to communicate with our inner child is bounded by our fear of imperfections, flaws, mistakes or appearing vulnerable. We choose to conceal and not feel. The persuasion of concealing our feelings or vulnerabilities can cause a rift with our inner child. When we were kids, we didn't pay attention to what others might think of us; we just did what we liked, had fun, sought joy, and played carelessly. But all of the fun and enjoyment abruptly ended in order to make way for adulthood, and we began to neglect our inner child in order to meet the many expectations of others in order to be accepted. We *want* to be accepted. We *want* to be appreciated. We are afraid that people might judge, discriminate and reject us. We want to feel like we belong. We want to be seen, and heard, so thus, we would always go for extra miles to please the people around us, putting up masks, displaying different personas while draining ourselves to be someone we are not in meeting people's expectations. Dr. Venetia Leonidaki, a consultant clinical psychologist who provides clinical leadership in the NHS stated that:

"Our desire to please other people and our fear that we will lose their love if we don't also result in neglecting our inner child. Neurobiology plays a role, too. Changes in certain areas of the brain, such as the prefrontal cortex, lead to new levels of sophistication in our thinking, which make us better prepared to regulate emotions and impulses. Our most sophisticated, grown-up, thinking capacity could make us rely less on raw emotions, which our inner child is mostly in touch with, driving us away from the childlike part of ourselves."

Society's toxic expectations, unhealthy cultural and societal norms had always pressured us and made us feel lacking. For example the common pressure exerted on women to settle down by the age of 30 while they refuse to understand the rationale and logic of why these women refuse to conform to such pressure. But somehow these expectations may influence us women in fulfilling them, causing us mental health deterioration and making us become oblivious to our inner child's joyful, carefree side. Furthermore, emotional trauma, such as childhood trauma stemming from generational issues, can leave us as adults with unresolved pain, making it challenging to reconnect with our inner child and embrace childlike qualities. Some people can embrace their inner child with openness because they had a healthy and safe childhood experience with the presence of responsible, empathic and caring adults. But some people have gone through traumatic childhood experiences, such as abuse, neglect, grief in losing a parent to illness, experiencing poverty, or witnessing their parents' divorce, so they are unable to process their emotions and find meaning in their pain and suffering. These people often experienced feelings of inadequacy and insecurity. Emotional wounds from past experiences, especially traumatic ones, can cause you to lose touch with your inner child. The inner child can be wounded or healthy, just like a physical child, bearing the weight of trauma, disappointment, and unfulfilled needs, and it can also convey joy, curiosity, and innocence. Dr. Venetia Leonidaki stated that:

"From early on in life, we need to strike a balance between the emotional needs that we feel inside and

the demands made or restrictions imposed by other people around us. Our parents, teachers, and later on our partners, employers, and children require us to show a responsible attitude, control our emotions, be rational, and conform to societal norms. As we constantly have to negotiate our internal needs with external pressures, we often end up suppressing and cutting off from our inner child."

Thus, this shows that we all have an inner child that has been shaped and moulded by our early experiences. Every action we take as adults is guided by a subconscious pattern that was ingrained in us as young children and subconsciously shapes who we are today. Most people are unaware of the fact that our adult decisions are influenced by the memories we have of our childhood. The stories we were told as children have an influence on how we set goals, act in relationships, and establish our own value. Our inner child is an essential part of ourselves and nurturing it can be a transformative step in our development.

Hence, the path to becoming our true selves requires revisiting our childhood wounds and viewing them through the lens of compassion and forgiveness. It needs us to pay attention to our vulnerable parts, which we have neglected. Such actions are related to self-transformation and self-improvement. If we healed our inner child, this would empower our adult lives. What's more to that is in understanding and nurturing our inner child is not only just about healing past wounds; it's about becoming a more authentic, confident, and fulfilled person in our lives who can recognise and love oneself. It's a journey that can also improve our social lives, communications, decision-making, and overall. By embracing and reconnecting our inner child, we can achieve not only greater self-awareness, but also a more genuine and meaningful presence in life.

Reconnecting with *The Inner Child*

Your inner child is more than just a bittersweet attachment to your past, but it keeps the memories of happiness, freedom, naivety and playfulness of childhood and our traumas, emotional wounds, and pain are also stored there. When we choose to reconnect with our inner child, we will start to work on being compassionate towards ourselves in understanding our inner? We will start to shelter our inner child in profound and empathic ways in order to assure that our inner child feels safe. When our inner child is protected, given a comfortable environment for it to run free, it will feel less threatening and more belonged and that is when the healthy, cheerful and joyful side of our inner child will resurface and find its way to shine and glow. Healing our inner child can help us face our hidden pain and aid us in addressing our past trauma.

Thus, reconnecting with and healing our inner child can be a potent strategy to support our emotional and psychological well-being. It holds the key to our present emotional well-being and potential growth. When we reconnect with our inner child, we unlock our curiosity, creativity, passion, resilience, joy, and ability to experience love, growth and compassion. It becomes a source of strength and a guide for living authentically. Reconnecting with our inner child is a transcending journey of self-awakening towards self-discovery, self-authenticity and growth. In the abundance of benefits of reconnecting with our inner child can contribute to our life, we also have to know that the process of connecting, nurturing and healing our inner child is a work in progress. It is an enduring process that demands patience and persistence. I had worked on a lot of ways in the past to reconnect with that little girl inside of me, and it took the changing of new ways to reach to a point where I felt connected with her. While I have also shared the personal self-tips in reconnecting with my inner child in my previous books, I would now like to share my current personal ways of reaching my inner child. I would like to share the five current personal tips which had welcomed me to my inner child and made me feel more belonged in life.

My 5 personal current ways to reach my inner child:

1. ACKNOWLEDGING THE INNER CHILD

I believe before we plan out any further steps to bring out the inner child in us, it is most important for us to know its existence within us. We need to know that there is an inner child being caged inside of us waiting to be freed. In knowing that a little version of us exists within the many layers in us could be the first realisation towards actions. I bet we all have our own imagination of what our inner child might look like. It might appear as a bubbly cheerful little one and it might also appear as a frowning little girl sitting under the cloudy sky. It might also disappear into the unknown of where we found it. Our inner child had tasted joy and fear and what we are encouraged to do now as adults is to face the fear and bring out the joy. This is not something breezy. Imagine we have to embark on an emotional exploration, visiting the hurtful parts of ourselves that we always run from, it would be greatly uncomfortable. But somehow it is impossible for us to reconnect with that inner child of ours if we are not aware of its presence, its existence, to recognise and acknowledge it as it is the first step towards embracing our inner child.

Thus, my first step in connecting with my inner child is to acknowledge that this part exists within me. Recognising and acknowledging our inner child's wounds and joy can allow us to break free from our toxic and vicious cycle, unhealthy thinking patterns and beliefs that may be holding us back to progress in adult life. To dive deeper into oneself and face our fears, to bring out the best parts of us and work on ourselves to not only heal but to transform. To have effort and doing the inner child work to change our situation towards betterment which is aligned with a verse in the Qur'an:

> *"Verily, Allah (s.w.t.) will not change the condition of a people until they change what is in themselves."*
>
> (*surah* ar-Raʻd, 13:11)

This verse has not only inspired but empowers those who are on a journey of healing and growth. It is an *ayah* that reminds us of all that our effort is worthwhile, and no effort will be in vain if it is intended for Allah (s.w.t.). This verse from the Qur'an speaks to the importance of our willpower, actions and effort and how we can change ourselves and our lives towards betterment, growth and success. Hence never underestimate your own power to reconnect with that inner child of yours in order to survive and thrive in life.

2. WRITE A LETTER TO THE LITTLE YOU

I could say this is my most favourite daily activity, a past favourite activity where I continued doing it until now. I love writing letters to my inner child, as I personally believe that writing letters to your inner child is a way for you to get to know yourself better. This is inspired by a classic Arabic proverb that states:

Whoever knows himself, knows his Lord.

(Ḥilyat al-Awliyā' 10/208)

The proverb implies a tremendous responsibility for knowing and reflecting on oneself in order to strengthen one's connection with God the Almighty. And in the many ways I've learned in the Islamic teaching, I also find that my personal routine of writing letters to my inner child has somehow reminded me more of the creation of myself and my Lord. When it comes to compiling my inner child letters, I even work on to share some of the written letters which do not appear too personal on my social media and witness how many people find it relatable and resonating. I sometimes think to myself whether our souls had actually met each other before we were born on earth. We nearly shared the same wounds, pain and scars and we are somehow here together on earth to support and be there for one another. We all forget who we are at times, and writing a personal letter to yourself can remind you of who you are from time to time as we all go through unconscious constant changes without us even realising about it. It can also help you to uncover the hidden wounds beneath adulthood, unveil the deepest pain and greatest fear that we have within us. Believe me there is a lot that we had missed and overlooked about ourselves since we started to venture into adulthood. There were so many things we tend to ignore and push away. It can actually be anything that suits your comfort to start off with and make it into a routine. Thus, writing letters to your inner child can be a great personal way to tap into that little version of you.

Writing your inner child a letter can even start with:

Dear little one,
I am in pain.
Yours truly,
The Adult Version of You

3. SPEND TIME WITH CHILDREN

Children are indeed innocent and pure; their sins aren't counted until they hit puberty in Islam. Allah (s.w.t.) created children so people can find ease when they engage with children. Children are a blessing for adults. Have you noticed sometimes being around a child will make you gravitate towards that inner child of yours? When was the last time you met, played and talked with a child? When you play or talk to a child the inner playfulness and cheerfulness of you naturally resurface to match the child's wavelength. Surprisingly having that childish part of you comes out becomes something that makes you feel at ease. Simply, you find joy in that day of yours.

Looking at children can give you a heart-warming feeling, you feel a kind of light-heartedness in seeing them play, giggling, actively running, talking in a cute and bubbly way, etc. Sometimes by just being around a child makes you smile, and our soul catches their child like energy. Children are truly blessed, as children heal the cracks in the adult soul. Children restore our youthful spirit. Being around children exposes us to the joys of play and warmth. We feel at ease snuggling with a child, and the nearness of their small bodies brings a soothing calm to our adult world. Thus, revealing the fact that there is so much we can learn from a child. Being with them reminds us to tap into that little version of ourselves. It teaches us to be free spirited and playful again, being with a child can activate our imagination and the inner child inside of us. Sometimes when we allow our inner child to run free, it becomes good for our adult mind and spirit. It inspires us to see joy in the little things in life and be grateful of our little achievements, for example when seeing how happy a child is just by being able to tie their own shoelaces or pronouncing a word correctly. Those are the little things they cherish.

There was a qualitative study conducted by Sjöblom, Ohrling, and Kostenius in 2018 which found that childhood experiences can teach us life lessons that help us adapt to situations across our lifespans, which characterises the essence of the inner child. Diana Raab, Ph.D. who is an expert in transforming and empowering people through creativity, stated that there are studies which have shown that we adults actually have a lot of things to learn from children and even infants. We have a lot to learn from their little world and their carefree soul. Children are always open to new things in their adventurous, creative and imaginative ways of exploring, discovering and learning. She mentioned that:

If all of us just stopped to see with a child's eyes, we might find that we also feel more joyful on a daily basis. Kids are figuring out everything during the course of the day. They have a heightened sense of awareness that allows them to pick up things we might miss, and, interestingly, this heightened sense might lead us to believe that they're smarter than we think.

Hence, there is a lot of magic we can feel from children and for that, children should be appreciated and they deserve to be treated with care, kindness and compassion. The Prophet's (s.a.w) nature of kindness and gentleness towards children is amazing and heart-warming. The way the Prophet (s.a.w) treated children is an example to us all. The Prophet (s.a.w) would show affectionate love to children by kissing and embracing children often, as an expression of his compassion towards them. In a hadith Abu Hurayrah (r.a.) reported that al-Aqra' bin Habis saw Allah's Messenger (s.a.w) kissing al-Hassan (the Prophet's grandson). He (al-Aqra') said: "I have ten children, but I have never kissed any of them". Whereupon Allah's Messenger s.a.w. replied:

> *He who does not show mercy (towards his children), no mercy would be shown to him.*
>
> (Ṣaḥiḥ Muslim 2318a)

In this hadith, we see the example of the Prophet (s.a.w.) who portrayed the importance of treating children with love and compassion. A combination of heartfelt playful activities, combined with loving conversations will provide security and comfort, thereby ensuring that a child and also an adult owns a stable emotional health and experience.

4. ENGAGE IN CREATIVE ACTIVITIES

I believe that gravitating towards creative activity can help us in discovering our inner child. When we engage in activities that are near to the human nature, it sparks the joy and creativity in us. When we choose to indulge in arts, literature, for example, it brings out the adventurous side of us, it ignites our passion and allows our imagination to run wild and explore new horizons. Thus, when did you last enjoy, ease, and joy from your creative endeavours? Children seem to be creative beings all the time. Without barriers or worries about making a mistake, they dive into exploration. Their carefree soul guided them to unpaved roads turning themselves into amateur painters, musicians, writers, dancers, thinkers, and creators. While in the adulthood, there is fear of getting a writing or a drawing ugly, looking silly, or a waste of time and energy, maybe we can learn from a quote from American author Mark Twain:

Sing like no one's listening, love like you've never been hurt, dance like nobody's watching, and live like it's heaven on Earth.

Maybe what we need is to become a child again at times, be playful and forget about the outcome. See the creative activity as a process of self-healing in expressing and liberating your pushed-down uncomfortable emotions. Try to also remember what your favourite creative activity was when you were little. Free your imagination and try to give it a go without worrying about the end result. Getting creative can help people to connect with themselves, with their inner child and also with the world, engaging with your senses and imagination can allow you to enter a creative flow, where the mind and body work together, being immersed in the creative task at hand and experiencing a feeling of peace and clarity. Know that our spirit and inner child wants to be heard, seen, valued, and appreciated. Regardless of people's judgements and societal expectations, we have to know that we are humans with a soul, not robots. We deserve to embark on a creative healing journey without furthering our pursuit of external validation.

5. READING BOOKS ON INNER CHILD

The moment I started to hear the term 'Inner Child' it drove me into discovering it. The term itself resonated with me. As a person who finds reading things that challenges the mind and drives the imagination wild and fascinating, I bought books on inner child and even read journals and articles on such topics. It's important to seek knowledge on things we don't know as it helps us to grow and become aware of the things in life. Islam places a high value on reading and encourages it as a way to learn. The Qur'an has emphasised the importance of knowledge and reading. In the very first revelation to the Prophet, it began with the command: "Read!". This points out how important reading and learning are. It is encouraged for Muslims to pursue knowledge in all areas of their lives, including the humanities, sciences, arts, and religious studies.

Prophet Muhammad (s.a.w.) said, "Seeking knowledge is obligatory upon every Muslim."

This shows how important it is to seek knowledge and learn.

Hence here I would like to share the two most favourite book on inner child that I had ventured on which are *Recovery of Your Inner Child: The Highly Acclaimed Method for Liberating Your Inner Self* by Lucia Capacchione which shares on showing you how to have a first-hand experience of your Inner Child, to feel its emotions and recapture its sense of wonder by writing and drawing with your non-dominant hand where Dr. Capacchione shares scores of hands-on activities that will help you to embrace your 'inner vulnerable child', your 'inner angry child', your 'nurturing parent' within, and finally discover the 'creative and magical child' that can heal your life.

The second one is titled *Homecoming: Reclaiming and Championing Your Inner Child* by John Bradshaw which shares on how your wounded inner child may be causing you pain, to validate your inner child through meditations and affirmations, give your child permission to break destructive family roles and rules and adopt new rules in incorporating honest self-expression to reconnect with your inner child.

Thus it is crucial to understand that part of the process of self-love, self-discovery, self-authenticity, emotional healing and growth is realising and accepting the inner child. Healing your inner child can change your life. You might also have a better relationship with yourself and others, as well as improving mental health condition, and general well-being after you addressed your inner child wounds and childhood trauma. Reconnecting with my inner child had worked wonders. I found that love revisits when you start holding hands again with that inner child of yours. Your inner child holds the magic to unleash love within your soul. It allows you to reconnect with the true you. Our inner child holds the power in enabling people to love oneself—in allowing you to reconnect with your genuineness, to resurface your originality and unveil your authenticity. It is indeed beautiful, when a person knows the presence of the inner child is to redirect and re-navigate a soul who had sailed too far from the right route. The inner child can be the twinkling stars above that aid a sailor across the sea in the darkest of the night.

It was said by Diana Raab, Ph.D that;

Being in touch with your inner child is a safe way to take a break from everything that's going on in the world. The inner child thinks positively and believes in the possibilities in everything. If you put yourself in "child mode," you may find that you become more open to the magnificent opportunities that exist all around you.

We learn on our inner fights, toughest battles, embarking on journeys towards healing and growth when we acknowledge the presence of our inner child, the musings it holds, the grace and innocent wisdom we offered the world when we were still children. Reconnecting with our inner child can go back to being our truest selves and permitting ourselves to love ourselves unconditionally, the way we were before the outside world influenced and defined us on who and how we should be. In my view, our inner child serves as our best mentor in life where they help us in leading with empathy and compassion while navigating life's waves. May your journey to meet your inner child be eased. And if one day you have finally joined hands with that inner child of yours, do send my regards to it. I hope that it may grow happier, more hopeful, and more faithful towards joyful and promising days.

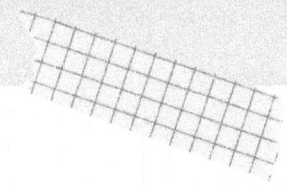

Dear self,

Thank you very much. Thank you very much for your presence in this world. Thank you very much for choosing to exist. Thank you very much for being who you are today. Thank you very much for working on your passion and interest. Thank you very much for finding yourself. Thank you very much for showing love and compassion to yourself. Thank you very much for surviving and thriving. Thank you very much for hoping and believing. Thank you very much for choosing to change in becoming a better person. Thank you very much for choosing to become wise. Thank you very much for choosing to persist. Thank you very much for believing in my potential and strength to continue to live. Thank you very much for having faith in me.

Thank you very much for being a loyal supporter in my healing journey and for believing that I will heal. Thank you very much for being patient with my transformation process. Thank you very much for believing that I can change into a better person and for making me grow closer to my Lord. Thank you very much for sincerely accepting all my flaws and shortcomings.

Thank you very much for your loyalty, transparency, and honesty. Thank you very much for becoming the muse for my comeback in empowerment and growth. Thank you very much for being the inspiration towards my aspirations. Thank you very much for your understanding and for wanting the best for me.

    Thank you very much for always reminding me to stay true to this path. Thank you very much for reminding me of my values, visions and missions. Thank you very much for always being the friend and sidekick during the ups and downs.

Lots of Love,

Your true self

*It's OK to be playful and
be a child sometimes*

*As it is not something to be
ashamed of nor it's a crime*

*Even if in the mirror we witness
our wrinkles and fine lines*

*Because that is a calling for your
inner child, it is a wondrous sign*

*For your inner child to be on loose
and magnificently shine*

*You'll soon embrace that little
version of you to be content and fine*

*This is the chance for your
adult version to be redefine*

*By the calling of love, hope,
faith and the divine*

ELIMINATING TOXICITY

On Toxicity

Toxic, in scientific terminology, is a designation applied to things that may be harmful, such as dangerous compounds and in this context, 'toxic' is a term for actions that are unpleasant or destructive toward other people. Toxic in human behaviour refers to a person who deteriorates other people mentally and physically with their constant destructive words and actions. While we can detect a toxic person easily, sometimes it can also be difficult to spot one because of their manipulativeness or psychopathic characters. For example, you can be constantly confused, anxious, or stressed out by a certain individual in your life, but you don't know why because they easily got away with it by gaslighting. We all have experienced meeting toxic people in our lives, or we will one day encounter such individuals in life as it's a part of life and it's just unavoidable. Whether it's a negative partner who mistreated you, a friend who doesn't value you and constantly takes advantage of you, a manipulative boss who controls you or an unhealthy working culture by a group of people that suffocates you, toxicity could make us feel inadequate to the point where the shame, guilt and pain drive us towards harmful actions. It may be mentally or physically abusive to communicate constantly with and stay in a relationship with toxic people as we have to know that the tendency of toxic people is to always want to dominate.

Toxic people can actually be harmful to your mental health and well-being, and can also have a detrimental effect on our self-esteem. Anyone whose actions bring constant stress and negativity into your life is toxic. People who are toxic would always project their fears and insecurities on others. They prey on our weaknesses, bring out the worst in us, or belittle us for their gain. They act in ways that often upset other people in the process. It can be upsetting and perplexing. It can even make you feel like you're the one to blame. Toxic behaviour is nonetheless harmful despite the possibility that there is an intention and purpose for it. It won't always be easy to remove yourself from toxic people in life, but believe me, with gradual progress it will be the best thing you can do for your mental and emotional well-being. It is said by Mufti Menk that:

Don't feel guilty about staying away from toxic people who cause you pain, insult you and disregard your feelings. They'll make you miserable.

In Islam human rights are extremely precious. Islam considers it sinful to harm another person. Nobody will be able to get away with their terrible conduct if they have oppressed someone or injured them in any manner. Allah (s.w.t.) considers the rights violations of His people. Hurting someone emotionally, or physically, is a serious sin in Allah's (s.w.t.) sight, and He alone will deal with it in this life and the Hereafter. Muslims must be cautious in their words and actions that might offend others, as Islam taught us to respect one another as human beings and not overly harm each other with our doings.

Messenger of Allah (s.a.w.) said:

The believers in their mutual kindness, compassion, and sympathy are just like one body. When one of the limbs suffers, the whole body responds to it with wakefulness and fever.

(Riyad as-Salihin 224)

The above hadith had highlighted how we should look after one another from mental or physical harm as Islam teaches us to be respectful regardless of our differences. We should be kind, not harmful in dealing with others, speaking of others and not bulldozing people's boundaries at our heart's wishes. Personal boundaries are restrictions we set for ourselves on a physical, emotional, and mental level to protect us from the hurtful words, poisonous energy, and negative emotions of others. Islam places a strong emphasis on personal boundaries and there are morality and integrity we need to abide with in engaging with people.

We have the right to protect ourselves from people who are highly negative, rude, aggressive, manipulative, narcissistic and dismissive towards you. They torture you despite your innocence, when you've done nothing wrong—it's not your fault. These toxic individuals are simply acting out of their own sense of inferiority towards you. And obviously this person has personal issues, and it has nothing to do with you. Thus, I want you to know that you can free yourself from such mental abuse, you can leave and turn away from the things which do not concern you, such as their words, their actions. It might be difficult at first, but the enduring process will be protecting your mental well-being. It is stated in the hadith that:

The Prophet (s.a.w.) said:

Part of the perfection of one's Islam is his leaving that which does not concern him.

(Sunan Ibn Majah 3976)

The truth is, it is important to consider the people you often spend time with, because they can highly influence you. Good relationships, whether with friends, family, or in marriage, provide genuine support, encouragement, and inspiration. On the other hand, toxic relationships normalise negative behaviours and can pull you into a harmful dynamic if you're not careful. In a hadith Prophet Muhammad (s.a.w.) stated that:

A man is upon the religion of his close friend, so beware whom you befriend.

(Jami' at-Tirmidhi 2378)

This hadith reminds us to be aware of the company we

keep. The integrity, morality and character of those you spend the most time with will be imposed onto you as well as the opposite characters of it, thus choose what weighs more towards the blessings of Allah (s.w.t.).

Acknowledging toxicity in a relationship

I believe it is my duty to protect myself against environments or individuals that might worsen my mental health and well-being. For some people their physical health will be affected when their mental health deteriorates, thus you should never put your mental health at risk for anything or anyone. It's crucial to avoid placing ourselves in toxic situations that rob us of our serenity and inner peace. It's never going to be worthwhile because in actuality, the toxic individuals that are the ones who will benefit from their actions if we still remain in the toxic relationship.

Moreover, Allah (s.w.t.) says in *surah* al-Baqarah, verse 195:

"...do not throw [yourselves] with your [own] hands into destruction.."

As I personally reflected on the *ayah* above, I learned that Islam tells us that one of the goals of *Shariah*/Islamic law is to safeguard a person's life, body, and mind. This is one of the fundamental elements of Islam. We are told by Allah (s.w.t.) that engaging in destructive and toxic behaviour is bad for your body and mind whether it is internal or external as each one often relates to one another. Engaging in toxicity will eventually lead to major destruction of oneself. I believe it is of utmost importance to guard us against the factors of toxicity. We can witness how people had lost trust and faith after they discovered the toxicity of a person either in a friendship, marriage or kinship. Toxic relationships can happen anywhere like at your workplace, at school, or even at your own home and it involves anybody, including colleagues, friends, and family members. A toxic relationship is a relationship that makes you feel degraded, discredited, unsupported, constantly misunderstood, and attacked. Any relationship that makes you feel worse or drained rather than better or joyful can turn toxic over time. To the wounded, unfulfilled, emotionally neglected, abused people who find any of their relationships (Friendship, marriage, kinship, among others) hurtful need help. Here are some significant signs of an unhealthy relationship listed by Roxy Zarrabi, Psy.D. who is a clinical psychologist specialises in helping women struggling with low self-esteem, anxiety, or relationship challenges:

1. You're not voicing your boundaries, needs, or feelings due to fear that you will be labelled negatively.
2. Multiple friends or family have expressed genuine concern about your relationship and the impact it's having on you.
3. You feel a growing discomfort about the relationship but ignore it or rationalise it by telling yourself that all relationships are hard work.
4. You feel the need to hide parts of your relationship when sharing with others due to fear of judgement.
5. You frequently feel anxious or on edge about your relationship.
6. You are over-functioning in trying to keep the relationship afloat, for the lack of effort they're making to make the relationship work.
7. The relationship often feels like an emotional rollercoaster.
8. You keep hoping the person you're with will finally change.
9. You don't feel emotionally safe in the relationship.

10. You are sacrificing your authenticity for the relationship.

11. You don't feel good about yourself in the relationship. You often feel judged by your partner and are full of self-doubt. You may even experience a lot of self-blame for anything that goes wrong in the relationship.

12. You notice that after you got into this relationship, you started to feel distant from your family and friends.

13. You often feel like you are walking on eggshells in the relationship.

14. Your boundaries (emotional, financial, physical, among others) are not being respected in this relationship.

Thus it is truly important to recognise and acknowledge a toxic relationship before we face further deterioration. The truth is it's never easy to escape a toxic relationship. When we hesitate between staying and leaving, others may judge our choices as unwise, unaware of our earnest pursuit of personal happiness. But I want you to know that you are not alone. I want you to know that there are also many people out there who share the same story with you. I just want to say that while you're not broken into pieces yet, while your heart is still in one piece and whole, here's the chance to reflect, contemplate, and gradually re-seek that inner strength within you to escape.

I believe that a pretty soul like you deserves so much more than peace and joyfulness. You deserve true love, genuine care, loyalty, honesty, sincerity, gentleness, trust, authenticity, and security. I want you to know that love is not only about the feeling itself, it's not only being happy around the idea of loving and being loved but it's about *how* to love and be loved. It's about choosing the right friend that will be with you through thick and thin, it's about choosing the right future father or mother of your child, it's about knowing how to mentally guard yourself against toxic kinship while not cutting ties. It's about living a fulfilling and content life ahead with a trusted person that will support, see, hear, validate and appreciate you. Sometimes we have to convince or encourage ourselves to start thinking about the future when including a person to be in our circle. Because the people we allow into our circle can have a big influence on our lives. The people in our circle can make us grow closer to the *deen* or the opposite of it. The people in our circle can inspire us to mend our bond with Allah (s.w.t.) or wreck it. So you ought to choose wisely who you let into your life.

I know, the more we want to hold on to it, the more it makes us question our sanity. We grew overwhelmed and felt uncomfortable with ourselves and due to it, we decided to silence our inner voice because it might be easier for some of us to just ignore the alarming inner voice which is shouting for help and care. *I know. I've been there.* Even though I could not fully understand, I could relate and feel more or less the same. But here is something that I've learned; anything that robs your inner peace and brings harm to your mental health will never be worth it. Paulo Coelho said that anything that costs your inner peace is too expensive, so let it go. Don't let people pull you into their storm but pull them into your peace, and if you are unable to do it, it's time for you to find your way out of it. And I learned it the hard way. I used to want people to love me without me trying to love myself first. I learned that we can't force a person to like us but we sure can try our best to allow ourselves to embrace the flaws within us, accept our own mistakes and grow to love ourselves better.

Every human being on this planet whether Muslim or non-Muslim, is in search of peace. The important element which a human needs the most for living is mental peace. Many psychologists and behaviourists argue that at the end of the day, the greatest human drive is mental peace. Of all the states of mind, inner peace is one that people desire most. Emotionally and mentally stable; it is the condition of being at peace with the world and oneself. Islam places a great emphasis on achieving inner peace to attain spiritual growth and connect with Allah (s.w.t.). The Qur'an describes inner peace as a state of tranquillity and contentment that arises from a deep sense of faith and trust in Allah (s.w.t.). The stated *ayah* below shows the importance of inner peace in Islam:

> *"Those who have believed and whose hearts are assured by the remembrance of Allah. Unquestionably, by the remembrance of Allah hearts are assured"*
>
> (*surah* ar-Ra'd, 13:28)

Allah (s.w.t.) is the best source of peace. Our inner and mental peace lies in the remembrance of Allah (s.w.t.). Allah (s.w.t.) is the Creator of the universe. Islam is the religion of peace and tranquillity. Islamic teachings lead to inner peace when people follow them as aligned to the Qur'an and sunnah. If we read and study the Qur'an and the way of life of the Prophet, we will be enlightened on the right way of living and how to attain inner peace through faith, prayer, and the remembrance of Allah (s.w.t.). It starts with the most basic thing such as greeting among Muslims. Muslims are prescribed by Allah (s.w.t.) to say '*Assalammu'alaikum*' whenever they meet with other Muslim brothers. The meaning of this Arabic phrase is "May Allah (s.w.t.) bless you with peace". Thus, Islam, ultimately benefits the minds with peace and calmness. Moreover, apart from attaining nearness to Allah (s.w.t.) in having our embark on spiritual growth, we also have to work on our personal magical ways in removing ourselves from toxic relationships and start working on our inner peace.

Here are some of the personal ways which I had embarked on:

1. HAVE A GOAL IN LIFE

When you have something that you love to do, something that you can focus on—like a dream—your heart, soul, mind, and your whole being would work on it. We all have our dreams. It may be establishing a company, pursuing your postgraduate study, being a professor, a well-known artist, or an international best-selling author. We all have something that we want to achieve in life. And if we could bring the hard work to the table, it would be marvellous. Your effort in making your dream come true can be one of the best ways to keep you company and help you stay away from the thoughts that would destroy you.

2. SPEND TIME WITH WHAT YOU LOVE

Something that makes you feel fulfilled, joyful and alive is what you need to pursue and do. What makes you get out of bed in the morning is what you should channel your energy to. Based on my experience, when you do what you love to do and follow your passion, magic happens! Healing and recovery happen. Doing what you love is therapeutic—it heals. I used to spend my days and nights writing to make me less anxious and in control again and it tremendously worked. I believe that if something makes your heart flutter, it is something worth going after.

3. BUILD A SUPPORTIVE CIRCLE

Sometimes all you need are people whose wavelength aligns with you, whose energy matches yours, whose words uplift one's spirit, whose compassion eases the soul, whose empowerment inspires one's will, whose vision sharpens the mind, whose mission broadens horizons, whose support strengthens the heart and whose presence fills your life with boundless warmth, joy, and purpose. Find people who can bring the best out of you, who can make you believe in yourself, and be with you throughout the journey.

4. THERAPY

When there is a time you feel you need professional help, please don't hesitate and feel embarrassed, there is nothing to be ashamed of when we need help. It's OK if you need therapy. It's OK if you need a counsellor, a psychologist or a psychiatrist to guide and aid you in staying away from toxic relationships as well as help you to navigate your way through the recovery journey. Nothing is lacking inside of you when you reach for mental health medical services in order to heal. Instead, you are doing something great for yourself and not brushing your ego.

Thus, I do hope we can all find our way in removing ourselves from toxic relationships. Furthermore, I would like to touch on the toxic people who create the toxic culture of a workplace, people who become the origin of the presence of toxic relationships at workplaces.

Toxic Culture at Workplace

We spend nearly half of our lives being at our workplace—mingling and engaging with the people at our place or colleagues, so if there is room, opportunity or chances for you to find a working environment that is non-toxic that would be a great thing for your mental and physical health. Your body and mind would be thankful to you for the rest of your lives. Easier said than done, the harsh truth is that there are many people who do not have a choice and they need a job for a living so any job would be enough for them to pay their rent, car and feed their family. And so, the people who are going through the tough and toxic days, I pray that Allah (s.w.t.) lifts all of your burdens and ease your heavy heart, *Inshā'Allāh* (s.w.t.). And know that in the Qur'an, Allah (s.w.t.) mentioned:

> *"Allah does not charge a soul except [with that within] its capacity..."*
>
> (*surah* al-Baqarah, 2:286)

This *ayah* is so profound and comforting because in Allah's (s.w.t.) wisdom, whatever trial comes your way is something that Allah (s.w.t.) has planned and which He has guaranteed you can handle. You will eventually realise that what you are going through is something you can handle. He knows what's in our heart and mind. Although the sadness is overbearing; although the times might be tough, but still whatever comes your way can be overcome with your unwavering hope and faith in Allah (s.w.t.). That is Allah's (s.w.t.) promise. Honestly, I personally find the *ayah* to be empowering and supportive in the midst of toxicity. The truth is facing toxic people and culture at the workplace are a part of life but that doesn't make the experience easy. We still feel overwhelmed, stressed out and burnout because we are humans. Humans are emotional beings who react to various emotional events, including discrimination, oppression, bias, favouritism, exploitation, and bullying, in the workplace.

I've gone through and witnessed toxicity in the working world—from underestimation, judgements, harsh & negative criticism, mental torture, witnessing people being body shamed and being sexually harassed, negative and gossipy co-workers, to tyrannical upper management. What I learned was that a toxic working environment can really sabotage your personal life and cause mental and emotional deterioration. In my previous job, when new scriptwriters joined the company, colleagues would place bets on how long the new hires would stay, which I found quite rude. Yes, I was that new scriptwriter. After being there for three months, I finally understood their working system and environment, which I found extremely unhealthy for one's mental well-being. However, for those who had been working there long enough, it seemed normal. They viewed it as a challenge, and anyone who refused to participate was considered weak.

For me, having to complete 30 episodes of summary writing in half a day was overwhelming. I witnessed a colleague's hands shaking while trying to eat her meal after completing such a ridiculous and inhumane task. Moreover, being mocked and verbally abused during idea presentations was part of their culture. Ideas were ridiculed, judged, shamed, and underestimated for their amusement, ego, and pride.

Witnessing a colleague being body-shamed, forced to skip lunch, and sleeping at the office to complete her heavy workload was far from normal for me. The company's indoctrination, portraying such inhumane acts as challenges that one must "man up" or "toughen up" to, is unethical, uncivilised, and falls far short of professionalism.

Besides being a scriptwriter, I also had worked for different job scopes at different working places. One of them was working as an optometrist from retail to clinical. This is when I encountered a senior co-worker who would always want to be in an unhealthy competition with me in terms of knowledge and skills. While me, as a junior colleague, I just wanted to learn not to compete in an unhealthy way. These senior colleagues would underestimate and use your lack of knowledge to attack and make fun of you. And even among the senior colleagues, there were also unhealthy competitions going on. Fighting over sales and customers, backbiting and gossiping was like *dhikr* over there. Praising bosses and seniors had been a routine to get promotions and a raise in salary. Unfair treatment among employees had been a trend. At one workplace, after just two weeks of working, my salary was downgraded. When I asked the owner, she said it was because of my lack of skills. However, I had clearly explained during the interview that I hadn't worked in 'the position' for two years and would need at least a month to catch up and relearn things. She had assured me she was fine with that and understood, but after the contract was signed, everything changed completely. I could also still remember that she had the heart to say, "*Employing you is just a gamble for me.*" where I was truly shocked. Eventually, I grew sick due to the overload of stress and quitted.

Emotional and mental stress can have a large negative impact on your physical health. If you are working in a toxic environment, you are more likely to get sick and many toxic environments will not grant you the proper time off to recover from your illness.

(Psychology Today)

The truth is, it is far from integrity and morality when the bosses or upper managers abuse an employee's rights or emotionally mistreat them. Negative behaviours like injustice, denying employees' right and overworking the employees and others are detrimental to employees or co-workers and damaging to the company's reputation. Not only does it not help build a good working culture or environment, it will also eventually hinder the development of the success of an organisation. Islam has forbidden and discouraged such ruthless acts towards another human which could hurt them and violate their human rights. Allah (s.w.t.) has mentioned in the Qur'an:

"And those who harm believing men and believing women for [something] other than what they have

earned [i.e., deserved] have certainly borne upon themselves a slander and manifest sin."

(*surah* al-Aḥzab, 33: 58)

Rather than going miles to destroy a sister or brother in Islam, we should actually be looking out for each other, showing respect and compassion for one another, supporting each other during difficult times, and taking care of the sisterhood or brotherhood bond in portraying social etiquette as Islam had encouraged on. There are more stories I could share to illustrate what toxic workplaces look like but I'll stop now. If some of you aren't sure or still confused while struggling to identify what toxic looks like in a working place, then you're encouraged to check out the signs online from an official trustworthy website or refer to a professional in your area in identifying and recognising your situation.

Previously earlier in the first paragraph, I did mention about people who had no choice but to stay in a toxic workplace environment but as much as I want them to leave and save themselves, I have to also understand the situation that we all went through especially during the post-pandemic. I understand we all don't have the luxury to go for what we want, and I've been there. It was not a great feeling. We felt suffocated, painful and confused, we felt like we wanted to run away but we couldn't because we were tied with no options. I know that we might question: "Am I the problem?" "Am I fragile and weak?" "Am I lacking and incompetent?" When you are placed in a toxic workplace, you might try to find faults and see the biggest problem in you. But you have to know the best way to handle a toxic workplace is to know and understand that you are definitely not the problem. It is the toxic environment culture that breeds abusers. Later on, the toxic mindset, the toxic way of thinking and the toxic way of treating people will soon be passed down throughout the company and become a toxic cycle.

There is only a small chance that the toxic working culture at your current workplace will change and due to that, the only possible way is to quit and find a new job. But again, this is often easier said than done because quitting a job may be a big risk taken. We would never know what would happen next—would we be employed again? Or are we risking being unemployed for the rest of our lives? We need a lot of thinking and advice from the people we trust and so in the meantime here are some steps you can take to make your workdays and your personal life more bearable from Kristen Fuller, M.D:

- Set boundaries for yourself: Always take a lunch break, not bring work home, set clear expectations, have friendships outside of work, and not share too many personal details at work.

- Find a good support system among co-workers: One important way you can weather a toxic work environment is to find one or two good friends you can trust in your workplace and offer each other support and a place to vent.

- Avoid the gossip, be nice to everyone, and keep your head down.

- Find a healthy outlet: Whether it's exercise, cooking, gardening, or church, finding a healthy outlet or hobby can help you get your mind off of work.

Hence, for the people who treat other people with disrespect and inhumanity, I want you to know that one day your loved ones, family, friends, daughter, son, niece, nephew, sister, brother or anybody close to you will enter the working world and would you like to see them receiving the same treatment that you gave to an innocent employer or employee? and succumb to low morale? I don't think people need to feel like they're entering the war zone because of the extreme inhumane pressure at the workplace; we don't need mistreatments that will add to the harm to people's mental health. To go against morals and ethics, being disrespectful, practising verbal abuse, and giving mistreatments don't seem right. What will happen to humanity? Are we only being selective when it comes to humanity? Or are we embracing the concept of advocacy as a whole?

I encountered an excerpt from an academic journal that said;

Moreover, when leaders abandon the tools of blame, shame, and sanctions for achieving results, and instead encourage intellectual risk-taking, accepting occasional failure as part of the growth process, employees become willing to dedicate their time to exploring new ideas. And, when problems arise, as they naturally do, leaders who come from a place of curiosity and vulnerability, instead of dictating the next steps for achievement, begin to reclaim employees' trust. These new lenses offer fresh perspectives, transforming obstacles into opportunities and cubicles from jail cells to welcoming spaces that foster ideas and relationships, breaking the cycle of previous workplace abuse.

(Slemp, Kern, Patrick, & Ryan, 2018).

Sometimes I would question myself why must a workplace become a war where people shed their blood and tears every time; where people succumb to the most inhume mistreatments? I do believe that we can surely be better. We can make a change if we want and are willing to do it. It's really heart-breaking to see people enduring the bad treatments that they don't deserve. I pray to Allah (s.w.t.) that there will be justice for those who are going through it and surviving it.

There were times when I questioned Allah (s.w.t.), "Why am I placed in places that cause me major distress and make me sick?". Sometimes I just want to live and work happily without the need to be tortured mentally. It's indeed a tiring cycle to face in the many phases of your life, but then I realise that every meeting that Allah (s.w.t.) had arranged was actually to teach me something valuable. *Very valuable.* The way I reflect on this is every time I witness toxic characters, I will learn not to become like them. Don't ever be like the people who cause harm to other people's mental health. I could feel that being kind and being human is way much worth it.

Having endured mistreatment, as a victim, you would be less likely to do the same to other people. And you don't want that to happen to other people, especially your loved ones. Let the mistreatment stop with you and make your experience of being mistreated as one of the biggest inspirations to spread kindness and help people out there to survive. Your story can be their guide out of their miserable life. Allah (s.w.t.) does not purposely put you in a situation without the pearls of wisdom that will come with it. Now that you know how bad it feels to be in a place that suffocates you; you could help people, encourage people and motivate them to find their way out of the mess and show them the way to a better life.

For me, there was a moment in life when I felt so down, lost, confused and scared. I wanted to run away and leave all the workload behind due to the torture I received. I felt so alone. But Allah (s.w.t.) is kind. He is the Most Merciful. He is the Most Compassionate. He led me to the people that understood my pain, people who didn't judge me and also helped me to escape from the world of toxicity. Great friends and a loving husband—these people whom Allah (s.w.t.) had brought into my life are the greatest blessings that I could ever receive. Allah (s.w.t.) says:

"And cooperate in righteousness and piety, but do not cooperate in sin and aggression. And fear Allah; indeed, Allah is severe in penalty."

(*surah* al-Ma'idah, 5:2).

I want us all to help people who are in need. I want us all to be kind to ourselves and be kind to others. I want us all to deserve a joyful and peaceful life. *Inshā'Allāh.*

I only now came to the realisation that it's crucial to look after both your physical and mental health since doing so is an investment you can make over the years of your life. After living my life for decades, I began to safeguard my bodily and emotional well-being. I made every effort to avoid toxic individuals and environments.

Eventually, I discovered what I really want in life and chased that.

I don't want to normalise something that's unhealthy for the mind and body.

Less harsh criticism, more guidance.

Less underestimation, more motivation.

Less competition, more cooperation

Less mental torture, healthier environment.

Thank you.

Dear you,

I want you to know that if you are seeing that this whole world is full of toxicity, I want you to also know that this world is also full of beauty. Yes, yes! Believe me. You just need to find the right environment and the right people to make you believe that this world is beautiful. As many as there are bad people in this world, there are also kind-hearted people in this world who love to do good, help others and smile a lot. You just need to discover these gentle souls! There are people who are even selfless and prioritise their loved ones or even sometimes the people in need. Life is not all about hardships and rainy days, there is also sunshine and joyful days. There are people of laughter, warmth and kindness out there waiting to be discovered, waiting to be reunited with you.

I know for those who are used to being trapped in a world filled with disrespectfulness, rudeness, mistreatment and emotional abuse, I bet it might be really difficult for you to trust and believe in people again, even if they seem good or kind because you went through the worst. But I want you to know that you deserve to be seeing a life full of lights and colours. You deserve to see a life full of hope, love and faith. I want you to be fearless and have courage in discovering these kind-hearted people and also the bright side of this wonderful life.

I know it may take some time, and the journey may be tough but believe it will be worthwhile. Trust me there is indeed more than enough room for happiness, joy, contentment and peace for you.

Yours truly,

The brighter side of the world.

*You are not a person that
should spread hatefulness*

In this temporary world

*But you should be radiating
kindness and gracefulness*

*You should not make
the innocence passionless*

*But instead you should have a soul filled
with wakefulness and faithfulness*

ACROSS DUSK TO DAWN

The Soul Who Struggled in Darkness

I had always written about my healing journey in most of my books as the recovery journey itself had inspired me a lot in my writings and allowed me to get in touch with the depth of my emotions and feelings. I believe memories are powerful, it gives you meaning and fulfilment in continuing to live our life. It leads you towards life learning episodes and guides you towards profound wisdom in becoming a better version of yourself. I believe we all have our own journey towards recovery, and I bet your healing journey has become a survival guide for others or any person who is close to you, or your story might as well become a companion towards those who feared and cried in the nights. Or maybe after you shared your story, you might probably feel less lonely knowing that there are people out there who shared the same experience like you do. They will reach you and say 'Hey, I feel you, I've been there too'. Thus, due to these reasons, allow me to share my story again on how I made my way through the terrifying darkness.

Honestly, I was that one girl who would just abide by every rule and practice commanded in the Islamic teachings without further query. I accepted and blindly followed everything without any slight curiosity of wanting to know the purpose of every commandment from Allah (s.w.t.). I did not know why we should believe in God, why we should be Muslims and why we should do prayers and fasting. And so, when I was 17 years old, I was set on a soul-awakening journey of endless exploration, continuous discovery, wandering and wondering in adventures where I started to grow curious and started to question my faith. I started to question whether Islam is the right religion or is there any religion out there which speaks truth and if God really exists. I want to know who God is. How do we know Islam is the right religion? How can we be sure the Qur'an was revealed by God? How can we know that Islam is not a mere tale created by mankind? What if there is only darkness and pitch blackness after death? It's like we would just die and there would be nothing. What if everything is a lie and we didn't even know about it? What if the prophets and angels were just made up stories? I started to question many things. My head was filled with heaps of questions daily. I explored books of different kinds. I started to read more about Islam in depth, devoured books on Islamic studies, theology, history and philosophy. I did a lot of online reading and research on academic journals and articles in dedication. But somehow there was one big mistake, there was a lack of guidance from the people of authority in my journey of discovery.

To be honest, during my initial journey in discovering the answers to my questions, I did ask the group of *naqibah* if they could refer me to a scholar on the topic of God's existence during a gathering event but somehow they perceived my condition as something disgraceful. In the eyes of my *naqibah* at that time, she saw me as a sinful person for questioning these things and I needed to repent. It was as if there was no room for thinking and merely accepting everything. I started to question my *ustadha*, *ustadh* and Islamic academician but eventually they failed to differentiate between the ill mental condition and my spiritual well-being (As I reflect back in time). They constantly relate every incident with *shaytan*'s whisper and most of them told me not to further question things. It was nearly impossible to find anybody who could understand my condition as they only made it worse by instilling fear in my heart for being misguided and sent to *Jahannam*. Eventually none of them could help me so I eventually struggled alone while I was wondering if there is something wrong with my *'aqidah* and I had no idea on how to see it as a mental condition (I had zero knowledge on mental health at that moment). These recurrent questions had always come to cause me severe anxiety where it became unbearable and since then life was never the same.

I often woke up from sleep with a depressing and empty feeling. I felt clueless, lost and confused. I even found it difficult to perform *ṣalah* as these thoughts came bugging and all together deteriorating my quality of life. It was mental torture as every day I fear that I might end up leaving the religion and don't believe in God anymore. I was in great turmoil, and I started to experience an existential crisis as I questioned reality. My head grew noisier; tons of questions emerged. How do we even know what is real and what's not? How do we know anything for sure? It was suffocating. Truly suffocating. My days were hopeless, useless and meaningless. I was extremely and negatively affected when it came to the topic of death.

When the topic of death arises, such as seeing a scene on the TV on how a Muslim is wrapped in the shrouds, or having to go visit someone who had passed away and even hearing about death made me fearfully triggered on doubting the existence of the hereafter. I become restless when people talk about the hereafter as it gives me the recurrent thoughts on assuring that the hereafter exist, and everything won't be pitch black and filled with darkness after one's soul leaves the body.

My thoughts were always racing. The thoughts and doubts had given me extreme fear. It made me become critical and sceptic of nearly everything. There were intense questions that had given me anxiety and depression and resulted in me to succumb to scrupulosity. Hence the curiosity that was lacking in guidance but filled with judgements from the people had turned into a disease and it robbed my inner peace. I couldn't find solace and tranquillity. I felt purposeless and meaningless. My heart ached everyday due to my persistent questioning on faith. I happened to be perceived healthy and functioning on the outside but the truth is I was sick inside; I was chaotic and hectic inside. These intrusive thoughts that had turned into a vicious cycle had really gotten the best of me, they had somehow overpowered me and the more I was forced to not think about these negative thoughts, the more it grew wild and stronger. The more I struggled to be liberated the more it held me back.

Honestly I did tell my family and friends about my situation but somehow, they don't really understand what I was going through. But still, I continued to perform prayers and make *du'a'* even though I had doubts in my heart and the never-ending confusion in my mind. I kept pursuing the journey in seeking truth and a way out of this mess. Deep down in my heart, I still had a feeling that Allah (s.w.t.) is real, and Islam is the true religion. I just need to be assured and affirmed. Honestly, I did seek and re-seek answers from the people of authority and somehow at one point I felt that the answers were answered with the most logical explanation but somehow the thoughts still won't go away. That was when I suspected things had gone beyond spirituality. It was an alarming mental condition and that was when my parents had become my saviour. In the midst of them not really understanding things clearly, they were there to accompany me.

As I entered my twenties, I found myself grappling with various personal issues—from financial and family matters to career, relationships, and studies. These challenges took a toll on my physical health and contributed to feelings of anxiety and depression as I struggled with existential crises and spiritual turmoil. I was possessed by unwanted invisible creatures. It was said that I was at the lowest point of my life, so I was easily disturbed by them. I could still remember waking up with panic attacks; shaking and trembling in fear, succumbing to uncomfortable feelings that breeds constant anxiousness, frequent palpitations and hyperventilating. Weird things happened to me as I grew hopeless of life. And even after I had gone to the Islamic spiritual centre and the 'creature' managed to be chased away still, my anxiety continued to persist and resulted in physical sickness. The severe acid reflux had caused irritable coughing and difficulties in breathing. I was diagnosed with severe stomach problems and was admitted to the hospital.

In my late twenties, I was given a compassionate soulmate. He is my husband, Anas, who, surprisingly, had shared the same journey of experience in facing existential crises and scrupulosity. I personally perceive what he had gone through was much more painful but somehow, he managed to regain hope and bounced back in life with a greater life mission and vision. How miraculous Allah's (s.w.t.) plan is for this beautiful meeting? Anas became a loyal supporter who had shown continuous patience and empathy when I was struggling in my path of recovery. I continued to visit health clinics and see doctors to get reassurance that I wouldn't die while I was learning to adjust to married life. I saw numerous specialists due to the condition, and eventually I was referred to a psychiatrist. After seeing several psychiatrists, getting the wrong diagnosis, having my medication tweaked, and experiencing depression from taking the wrong medication, I was finally given the correct diagnosis along with the right medications. My psychiatrist diagnosed me with general anxiety disorder and obsessive-compulsive disorder.

Until I discovered what was truly wrong with me, I spent my entire life believing that I was being cursed for misfortune. Almost no one closest to me knew anything truthful about mental illness before I met Anas, as there is a stigma that they attach to these kinds of illnesses. People with mental illnesses were often perceived as weak and delusional making it difficult for me to find a way to seek help. However, once I met Anas, he shared with me numerous incredible people who endured and survived mental illness. God is merciful. He led me down challenging paths and, at the end, pleasantly surprised me with a wonderful, warm gift. Anas was the guide who led me to the answers and solutions. He is the muse and inspiration. He had always found the pursuit of knowledge to be an enjoyable endeavour. He had a strong interest in academia and made me feel like I was stepping into a whole new world of enlightenment and knowledge. Anas taught me a great deal of things that have changed the way I think about and look at life.

Things I learned from Anas about life:

1. HAVING A MENTAL ILLNESS DOES NOT MAKE YOU LESS OF YOURSELF

Having a mental illness can sometimes make you feel inferior and less confident. We might also have a lack of faith in ourselves. In the past, I would always doubt myself. I would harshly criticise myself. I would hate myself. I would belittle myself. I wish that I was normal and was not diagnosed with the illness. Besides people's judgement, I added my own judgement. I would always think about myself in a negative way and never imagined a bright future with myself having this condition. But now I know that I am worth it. The fights and battles that I went through were worthwhile and they made me more worthy of life. It made me deserve a better life—one that is full of love and laughter. A life that is made of my dreams and goals. I aspired to be someone that could make changes to the world when I was a kid; the dream got lost in the journey but now the dream comes again to greet me with hope. A hope that makes me believe in myself. A hope that tells me that my mental illness is not an obstacle but it is a stepping stone for me to thrive in the wilderness. If you have a mental disorder or a mental illness, I hope you won't feel less of yourself. You have to know that you're not hopeless. You are not an outcast. You are not trouble. You are not weak. You're worth it. You are a noble soul. You are precious.

> *"Your souls are precious, and can only be equal to the price of Paradise, so do not sell them for anything else."*
> (Imam ʿAli bin Abi Ṭalib (r.a.))

In *surah* aṭ-Ṭin verses 4-6, Allah (s.w.t.) says:

> *"We have certainly created man in the best of stature; Then We return him to the lowest of the low, Except for those who believe and do righteous deeds, for they will have a reward uninterrupted."*

Allah (s.w.t.) had told us in the Qur'an that you and I were made in the best of forms with the highest stature. We were endowed with extraordinary abilities and made better than the material possessions or things we yearn for.

Moreover, in *surah* Ali 'Imran verse 110, Allah (s.w.t.) says:

"You are the best nation produced [as an example] for mankind. You enjoin what is right and forbid what is wrong and believe in Allah."

The definition of true dignity and stature differs greatly from the definitions we use on a regular basis to value other people. Only when we judge our own and that of others using the blind and temporary do we truly devalue ourselves below our true and God-given nobility. Thus you are a noble soul and you can be someone useful and contribute to the community. Yes, it is absolutely possible. In the past, when I was battling and struggling like crazy and fought with all my might with my anxiety disorder, there were people who saw me as a burden. I was always sick and these people did not like to see or hear about me often being sick. I would sometimes feel useless but then Anas introduced me to the influential people in history that have a mental illness but were still successful. Soon after

I began to read about them. These people created history and inspired people with their talent and intellect.

Written by the *Northern Lakes Community Mental Health Authority,* this article sourced from the *National Alliance on Mental Illness* (www.nami.org), discusses the mental health struggles of several renowned historical figures. Ibrahim Lincoln, the revered sixteenth President of the United States, suffered from severe and incapacitating depression that occasionally led to thoughts of suicide, as documented in numerous biographies by Carl Sandburg. Isaac Newton, the scientist's mental illness is discussed in *The Dynamics of Creation* by Anthony Storr and *The Key to Genius: Manic Depression and the Creative Life* by D. Jablow Hershman and Julian Lieb. Michelangelo's mental illnesses—he is one of the world's greatest artistic geniuses—is also discussed in *The Dynamics of Creation* by Anthony Storr. Vincent Van Gogh, the celebrated artist, is known to have had bipolar disorder as discussed in *The Key to Genius: Manic Depression and the Creative Life* by D. Jablow Hershman and Julian Lieb and *Dear Theo, The Autobiography of Van Gogh.* Last but not least, Charles Dicken, one of the greatest authors in the English language suffered from clinical depression, as documented in *The Key to Genius: Manic Depression and the Creative Life* by

D. Jablow Hershman and Julian Lieb, and *Charles Dickens: His Tragedy and Triumph* by Edgar Johnson.

The stated above are only some of them that I used as examples just to show you that we can all be successful. We can all reach the stars. There's a huge possibility of making your dreams come true.

2. IT'S OK TO QUESTION

I know when we are unclear about something, we tend to be curious. Throughout my years as a student, from childhood to adulthood, the courage or the habit to question was always praised by teachers or educators. It was a good thing and highly encouraged for students to be curious about the subjects we learned. But when it comes to our faith, I know not many of us were encouraged to ask questions about religious doubts. We are told to just stop questioning when it comes to our faith and just follow everything so we will not cause problems to our ʿaqidah. This is why whenever we have questions, we become worried. We are afraid that we might anger Allah (s.w.t.) and we thought that questioning means no longer wanting to be Muslim. *I was like that.*

I could still remember when I was in an Islamic event and I asked one of the sisters over there who was a *naqibah* of another *usrah* group, about religious doubts. I truly believed that she understood the confusion and problems I'm dealing with and assumed that she had gone through what I'm experiencing at the moment. I was too naïve to assume a *naqibah* should understand better. However, her expressions totally changed after hearing my questions. It was as if I've committed the gravest sin on earth. Even the other sisters in the gathering looked at me in shock. I saw the *naqibah*'s brows furrowed, and with a serious face filled with disappointment she told me to not question and accept things as it is. She told me that my questions were dangerous to my *'aqidah* and faith and that I might stray away from Islam. The truth is I was not against Islam; I was just an innocent soul seeking for answers. The people around me also had no answers and they don't have this messy way of thinking like I had so this makes the answers seeking journey a little bit difficult. But soon Allah (s.w.t.) sent Anas to me.

And I learned that it's OK to ask questions. It's OK to ask about something that you don't know. It's OK to seek answers. Don't be afraid to ask, even the answer to the most absurd or ridiculous question can somehow lead you to certainty in life.

We have the right to explore and discover but make sure you are well-guided by people of authority. Asking questions about your doubts on your religion does not mean you are no longer Muslim. To question is not a sign that you're leaving Islam. To ask questions does not signify that you are deviating from the right path. No. But to ask and relearn is a way to expand your knowledge; it is a way to be firmer on holding to our faith and beliefs. It is a way to be more certain about our religion. Ponder, wonder, reflect, contemplate. The Qur'an makes it very evident that one should look for and examine the universe's signs of truth. The Qur'an often describes signs or tells the wise stories of the past people and asks its readers to think.

The Qur'an clearly encourages the observation and study of the signs of truth in the whole universe. It also criticises the actions of those who do not apply their intellect to distinguish between right and wrong. The Qur'an references people with minds and the ability to understand the truth numerous times. However, in certain verses, the Qur'an condemns those who ignore warning signs or adhere to cultural norms without question, as well as people who do not reason or use their intellect. Such individuals lack one of the most fundamental aspects of humanity, and their impure behaviour is caused by a lack of reasoning. The Qur'an encourages reasoning and emphasises its value. It repeatedly calls on people to use their intellect to choose the correct path. This is mentioned in the Qur'anic verses:

> *We will show them Our signs in the horizons and within themselves until it becomes clear to them that it is the truth...*
>
> (*surah* Fuṣṣilat, 41:53)

> *Say, [O' Muhammad], "Travel through the land and observe how He began creation. Then Allah (s.w.t.) will produce the final creation [i.e., development]. Indeed Allah (s.w.t.), over all things, is competent."*
>
> (*surah* al-'Ankabut, 29:20)

> *Do they not see the birds controlled in the atmosphere of the sky? None holds them up except Allah (s.w.t.). Indeed in that are signs for people who believe.*
>
> (*surah* an-Naḥl, 16:79)

> *Indeed, in the creation of the heavens and the earth and the alternation of the night and the day are signs for those of understanding—Who remember Allah while*

standing or sitting or [lying] on their sides and give thought to the creation of the heavens and the earth, [saying], "Our Lord, You did not create this aimlessly;..."

(*surah* Ali-'Imran, 3:190-191)

There was certainly in their stories a lesson for those of understanding

(*surah* Yusuf, 12:111)

...Thus do We explain in detail the signs for a people who give thought.

(*surah* Yunus, 10:24)

And it is He who spread the earth and placed therein firmly set mountains and rivers; and from all of the fruits He made therein two mates; He causes the night to cover the day. Indeed in that are signs for a people who give thought.

(*surah* ar-Ra'd, 13:3)

[We sent them] with clear proofs and written ordinances. And We revealed to you the message [i.e., the Qur'an] that you may make clear to the people what was sent down to them and that they might give thought.

(*surah* an-Naḥl, 16:44)

Do they not contemplate within themselves?...

(*surah* ar-Rum, 30:8)

And it is not for a soul [i.e., anyone] to believe except by permission of Allah, and He will place defilement1 upon those who will not use reason.

(*surah* Yunus, 10:100)

...Say, "Produce your proof, if you should be truthful."

(*surah* al-Baqarah, 2:111)

Who listen to speech and follow the best of it. Those are the ones Allah has guided, and those are people of truthful.

(*surah* az-Zumar, 39:18)

As per its enlightening teachings, the Qur'an consistently clarifies the fundamental principle guiding its laws and commands. Concepts like knowledge, reasoning, and thought are discussed nearly a thousand times in the Qur'an, suggesting that Islam is a deep and firm ideology that is very different from superstitions—Islam is based on logic and reasoning. The Qur'an outlines the fundamental truths and the reasoning that supports them. Thus, it is OK to question, explore and study. Below are some of the excerpts from an article on Yaqeen Institute in the Psychology & Mental Health: General Psychology on *Faith in Mind: Islam's Role in Mental Health* written by Dr. Osman Umarji, Director of Survey Research and Evaluation and Associate Editor and Dr. Farah Islam, Director of Psychospirituality Studies and Associate Editor.

Religious doubt refers to feelings of uncertainty towards, and a questioning of, religious teachings and beliefs. The experience of religious doubt can push a person into a deep existential crisis if not properly addressed.

When we turn to the Prophetic tradition, we find that the companions often felt distressed when experiencing doubt and sought guidance from the Prophet (s.a.w.). Therefore, we find numerous prophetic narrations

> *affirming that Muslims do experience religious doubt, and that this is normal and far from blameworthy. A companion once came to the Prophet (s.a.w.) and said, "O' Messenger of Allah (s.w.t.)! One of us has thoughts of such nature that he would rather be reduced to charcoal than speak about them." The Prophet (s.a.w.) replied, "Allāhu Akbar! Allāhu Akbar! Allāhu Akbar! Praise be to Allah (s.w.t.) who has reduced the evil of the devil to only suggestions and whisperings.*
>
> (Sunan Abu Dawud 5112)

In this narration, we see the distress that religious doubt brought upon the companion, yet we also see how the Prophet (s.a.w.) acknowledged the doubt and praised the companion. We learn that when we're faced with doubts, we need to tackle them head on by seeking Allah's (s.w.t.) protection and clarity on the questions with which we're grappling. This is how we bolster our *yaqin* (certainty).

Hence, dear restless souls, fear not in becoming a thinker, an adventurer and an explorer as it is encouraged for us by Allah (s.w.t.), The Utmost Kind to use our minds in seeking the ultimate truth and embrace the beauty as He absolutely understands. We have to seek for our life's faith to be rooted in us and for our meaning to be found.

3. THE STORY OF PROPHET IBRAHIM: A JOURNEY OF SEARCHING GOD

The truth is the journey in seeking Allah (s.w.t.) is never an easy one. Most struggle to learn about God, Islam and the *din*. The path of finding truth is indeed a challenge like how Prophet Muhammad (s.a.w.) had said:

> *The Paradise is surrounded by hardships...*

(Ṣaḥiḥ Muslim 2822)

People seek God in many mysterious ways; on different paths and roads, experiencing a variety of emotions and feelings as there are no definite ways that fit all people. We all have our personal journey of transcendence. We are all different in terms of understanding and there are many ways for a person to learn about something. A person who believes that beyond all creations, there should be a Creator, a God worthy of worship and is on the journey to know God, will explore and discover many paths. The same goes to our Prophet Ibrahim (a.s.) when he realised that a powerful force exists in the creation of everything, including the Earth and the heavens. He believed that the gods his people worshipped did not shield them from poverty or hunger, were incapable of creating anything at all, and could not even protect themselves. Thus, Prophet Ibrahim began contemplating on the creation of God, whom he did not yet know, but he strongly sensed the sovereignty of a mightier force and began his quest for God. Ibrahim made it his mission to seek the Lord. Initially, as he started to look up at the sky, he saw a large star and exclaimed, "This is my Lord." However, the star soon set and vanished as night fell. Ibrahim was taken aback, wondering how we could accept a God who vanishes with the arrival of night. Ibrahim persisted in his search until he noticed the moon in the sky. Thinking that this was the God he sought, he continued, but neither the moon nor the star survived longer than the dawn. Prophet Ibrahim became more hopeful upon seeing the sun, believing that this was the God he had been seeking. However, our dreams do not always come true. Prophet Ibrahim's hope was dashed when the sun set. He experienced disappointment and hopelessness until the God he sought led him to the authentic faith and sent his revelation, revealing that God had selected him to be a prophet and a warner for his people. This is the God that Prophet Ibrahim was searching for; it was Allah (s.w.t.), the One God, the Creator of Heaven and Earth, not the sun, the moon, not even the idols that his people worshipped. Hence, this is Prophet Ibrahim's story as told by the Holy Qur'an:

Thus did we show Ibrahim the kingdom of the heavens and the earth for him to be one of those who know (have Faith) with certainty.

When the night covered him over with darkness he saw a star. He said: "This is my lord." But when it was set, he said: "I like not those sets."

When he saw the moon rising up, he said: "This is my lord." But when it set, he said: "Unless my Lord guides me, I shall surely be among the people who went astray."

When he saw the sun rising up, he said: "This is my lord. This is greater." But when it was set, he said: "O' my people! I am indeed free from all that you join as partners (in worship, with Allah (s.w.t.)).

> *Verily, I have turned my face towards Him Who has created the heavens and the earth, as Hanifa (Islamic Monotheism, i.e. worshipping none but Allah (s.w.t.) Alone), and I am not of Al-Mushrikun (the ones that associates partners with Allah (s.w.t.), in worship)".*
>
> *His people disputed with him. He said: "Do you dispute with me concerning Allah (s.w.t.) while He has guided me? I fear not those whom you associate with Him (Allah (s.w.t.)) in worship. (Nothing can happen to me) except when my Lord (Allah (s.w.t.)) wills something. My Lord comprehends in His Knowledge all things. Will you not then remember?"*

(*surah* al-An'am, 6:75-80)

Thus, we can understand that even a prophet embarked on a journey of seeking his Lord. Therefore, I believe there is nothing that we should fear or judge when it comes to questioning and searching for truth and faith, as I strongly believe that we are people who think and read. What I have learned is that many of us can agree that using proper scientific reasoning is the only path to discovering the truth about Allah's (s.w.t.) creation and qualities. Since all things have a cause and an action, nothing can be an exception to the general rule that nothing appears out of the blue or occurs without a reason, as everyone acknowledges this. There are numerous clear examples of that. Everything in the universe was created from nothing, including everything that is mobile and everything that is non-living. The universe was created by someone, whether that someone was Allah (s.w.t.) or the Creator, a fact supported by science and common sense. It would not change the fact that the whole universe gives enough evidence for the existence of the Creator. Hence, try to search and do your best to seek and know Him, as it is truly a great pleasure upon truly acknowledging and recognising Allah (s.w.t.).

4. IMAM GHAZALI'S RESEEKING JOURNEY

During the height of the Muslim Golden Age, Imam al-Ghazali was a professor at the Nizamiyah University of Baghdad, which was regarded as one of the most esteemed and well-respected academic institutions. The renowned Islamic scholar made numerous contributions to the world, and his impact was profound and influential. People in positions of authority all over the world used his books as references. From the book *Deliverance from Error*, Imam al-Ghazali has inspired me the most and given me hope during times when I experienced existential crises and scrupulosity.

The book taught me that Imam Ghazali was a voracious reader who loved learning new things. He was an accomplished scholar in a wide range of subjects, particularly Islamic studies. Years went by, and after delving into the depths of human knowledge across all domains, he suddenly began to doubt almost everything in life. He asked questions concerning religion, God, and faith. He even questioned the truth, logic, dependability, and rationality of his own mind. His mental and spiritual state had been severely disrupted by this terrible moment of darkness in his life. He was so consumed by inner turmoil that he stopped talking. After the illness worsened for a while, he made the decision to go in search of the remedy for his inner illness and set out on an adventure. He gave up his academic endeavours and worldly interests to live as a wanderer.

On his quest to discover reality and truth, he encountered four social groups. The first group was 'The Mystics'. He discovered that there were significant issues in their practice that were not aligned with the Islamic faith in many ways, and their source of reference would always be their "Shaykh" (leader). Next, he met 'The Philosophers', whom he eventually found problematic because some of their beliefs were not aligned with the Islamic faith. Then, he gathered with 'The Scholastic Theologians', where he knew that for some people, this would be the right group for them to find a cure and solace, but somehow, they were not for him. Finally, he joined the group of 'The Sufis', where the Sufis offered him a different quality that brought him serenity. Thus, this was a time of mystical personal transformation. He was given "Kashf." The Sufis proved to be the most suitable group for him; his illness was cured, and he was able to discover truth and reality at last. *Ihya' 'Ulumuddin* was born from there. He returned to his teaching duties but later resigned and lived alone for a while, writing books and reflecting on life. This led to the authorship of several timeless books.

Hence, what I personally reflected on al-Ghazali's life in the book *Deliverance from Error* is that even the greatest scholar in history went through these confused moments in life, but he chose to embark on a journey of exploration, thinking, and discovery in finding the truth and answers, showing that I am not alone and there is hope for me to seek light, inspiration, enlightenment, and comfort again.

5. *SEEK HELP*

Don't be afraid to reach for help. You don't have to be ashamed of your condition. There are many more things to be ashamed of in life, but to seek help regarding your health is not one of them. To seek help in order to save yourself is necessary. It's essential. It's crucial. It's a must. It's for the sake of your life. I know sometimes when it comes to prioritising our mental health we can be seen as selfish, or weak, or intentionally seeking attention but the truth is, you are just innocent and in need of a hand to reach for you and pull you back up. If you could convince yourself that you matter more than the thoughts of others, I want you to be kind to yourself and bring yourself to the hands of people that can aid you for better treatment. Deborah Serani, Psy.D., is a psychologist and psychoanalyst who lives with depression and specialises in its diagnosis and treatment. She said that;

> *People who struggle with asking for help often feel inadequate or insecure. They may worry that they're weak if they ask for help. Or they'll be viewed as powerless or inept. Or worse: damaged. Among the negative influences that can make help-seeking feel so*

uncomfortable are public stigma and self-stigma. Public stigma refers to the way society holds negative beliefs about "asking for help." Particularly when it comes to mental health, the long-standing stigma attached to seeking psychotherapy leads many to feel as if they're sick, crazy, or lazy. Despite science showing that mental illness is grounded in neurobiology, some people still wrongly assume that people who seek psychotherapy are weak, deranged, and dangerous. Self-stigma, the way one devalues oneself, may result from a person internalising other people's negative beliefs. Self-stigma lowers self-esteem and results in a person self-labelling as being socially unacceptable if they seek psychotherapy.

Meeting a counsellor doesn't mean you are a failure; meeting a psychologist doesn't mean you're damaged; meeting a psychiatrist doesn't mean you are crazy—this is an old stigmatised way of thinking which is totally wrong. But meeting the professionals is a bright way to lead a better life. They can give you new insights, an abundance of unknown information, a sea of knowledge, correct methods in navigating your life towards a better life. I hope you will not miss the chance or the opportunity to heal and live a great life. Below are the tips from Deborah Serani, Psy.D. in how to encourage a loved one or a friend who struggles with mental health issues but refused to seek for help:

a. Listen: Let your loved one or friend talk about what the struggle is, what symptoms are occurring or how they're coping with life. If they're resistant to sharing, be supportive by not forcing therapy as an ultimatum.

b. Respond: Let your loved one or friend know you're concerned about their well-being. Tell him or her that you understand the reluctance right now to see a professional mental health counsellor, but that you'll likely offer the suggestion of psychotherapy again.

c. Set up check-ins: Touching base by phone, text or email can be a good way to check-in on your friend or loved one. You can casually monitor the situation, but make sure not to overwhelm them (or yourself) with the goal of psychotherapy.

d. Seek psychotherapy yourself: If you're deeply concerned, you might want to seek a consultation with a mental health professional yourself. The therapist can help you formulate a more strategic plan for helping your loved one get help. Or aid you in accepting the limitations your friend or loved one has placed on your interventions.

e. Have an emergency plan: While you may not be able to get your loved one or friend to a mental health specialist, know that you can still intervene if necessary. When an emergency arises, like self-harm, suicidal thinking, psychotic breaks, delusions or risk taking behaviours, you can always call 911 and have the police bring your loved one to the nearest hospital emergency room. From there, they will get the mental and medical attention they need.

6. FIND THE RIGHT COMMUNITY

I understand that sometimes we prefer to be alone, walk alone, and live alone because we are more comfortable that way. It may also feel safer—I know it's really hard and difficult to trust people nowadays. Trusting takes all of our being sometimes, and it's really tiring when we are disappointed often. I used to be like this too. I preferred to live my own life without associating or engaging with people. I found it comfortable that way. Especially since I got married, living without a group of people made it easier because I knew I had my husband with me all along. However, as time passed, I started feeling lonely and unfulfilled, which caused me to feel the need to meet and talk with people. Despite this, I am still afraid of meeting the wrong people and establishing bonds with them.

> *On the flip side, loneliness is one of the biggest plagues in our society. It changes our thoughts and increases our levels of cortisol (stress hormone), which erodes our quality of life, sleep and overall health and well-being. It can affect our judgement and drive us to the brink of suicide, bringing on a crisis and even violence. In a world where we are ever connected, we are increasingly disconnected, finding ourselves without a community, without a "village," and without even a large enough circle of friends.*
>
> (Noor Suleiman, Writer at Haute Hijab)

Anas told me that you don't need to be with the whole world, where some people will give you unpleasant gestures, uncomfortable treatments, and make you feel unwelcome.

Instead, you just need to find the right group, the right community that can be your strong support system, your source of inspiration, your role models, where you can grow and thrive magnificently.

It was at this particular time, at this moment, that I started to find the right people whose values, faith, and life principles aligned with mine. I want my circle to be filled with people of kind hearts and empathetic souls, and *alḥamdulillāh*, I found a few communities that have changed my life in many ways. I am so thankful to Allah (s.w.t.) for the meeting.

First is the TRUE Islamic community, where I searched high and low to find non-judgemental Islamic groups that would lead me to the remembrance of Allah (s.w.t.). Being with these people always reminds me of Allah's (s.w.t.) mercy and blessings. My heart feels less restless and anxious. These groups always reach out to the needy and spread peace and kindness in the name of Allah (s.w.t.). One of these groups is *usrah*, an Islamic circle where the sisters sit together in a circle and share Islamic teachings and Qur'an reflections.

Besides sharing and reflecting, the sisters in *usrah* can be your support system. They can help you heal from heartbreak, keep going in life, devote yourself fully to Allah (s.w.t.), relearn Islam, be moved by a verse from the Qur'an, and meet the light again. Because in *usrah*, that's how things are supposed to work. We were taught to care for one another, to give emotional and mental support sincerely. Our friendship is for the sake of Allah (s.w.t.), *ukhwah fillāh lillāhi taʻala*.

> *But... imagine a world where at least once a day, you had the opportunity to connect with a brother or sister in faith. Where the girl who made the decision to take off her hijab can still walk into her masjid and get the same enthusiastic "Salam!" she used to get when she wore it. Where the boy who did drugs earlier this week can still feel like he can turn to Allah (s.w.t.) amongst his brothers in Islam. Where the woman who just miscarried can find love and support on any given day at the masjid. Where the man who just lost his job and has no family around can find compassion and maybe even some comic relief amongst his congregation to make a hard day a little less hard.*
>
> (Noor Suleiman, Writer at Haute Hijab)

In Islam, we are taught that it is important for us Muslims to play a role in the community. When we connect with our brothers and sisters, we get to know one another, we get to learn from one another and establish bonds. We also celebrate the teachings of Islam where we should help one another. We should help the brothers and sisters who are in need of our help. We should give a helping hand to the people who are going through hardships and worldly tests. Prophet Muhammad (s.a.w.) taught the Muslims to help one another and love one another and advise one another.

And, perhaps the most beautiful example of community in our history is when the Muslims migrated from Makkah to Madinah, and the Ansar (the people of Madinah) literally shared their homes, money and lives with the Muhajiroon (the migrants who came from Makkah). That is one of the most selfless acts a group of people could do for one another. This is all to say that community and community support is held in the highest regard in Islam and is something we all should prioritise in our lives.

(Noor Suleiman, Writer at Haute Hijab)

Every time when I walk through the stories of the ṣaḥabah and the people of Islam who lived in Prophet Muhammad's (s.a.w.) era, I would always encounter kind souls who sacrifice for the sake of their brothers and sisters. There were people who were willing to give shelter to the oppressed, lend their clothes to the needy and share food with the poor. The Prophet Muhammad (s.a.w.) would always teach the people to prioritise their brothers and sisters. It is indeed a noble teaching.

The Prophet Muhammad (s.a.w.) said:

A believer to another believer is like a building whose different parts support each other. The Prophet (s.a.w.) then clasped his hands with the fingers interlaced while saying that.

(Ṣaḥiḥ Bukhari 2466)

He (s.a.w.) also said:

The believers in their mutual kindness, compassion and sympathy are just like one body. When one of the limbs suffers, the whole body responds to it with wakefulness and fever."

(Ṣaḥiḥ Muslim 2586a)

My heart fills with warmth at the sight of witnessing

genuine acts of kindness. It's like my soul has been embraced with light and love. Now true peace is found. It's to be in a true Islamic community that cares for you like a family and also makes you feel safe and sound.

Next is the mental illness awareness or mental illness support group. I found these people in one of the biggest and most well-known mental illness awareness organisations in Malaysia which is MIASA. MIASA stands for Mental Illness Awareness and Support Association. MIASA is the leading voice in mental health education in support of people with mental health disorders. They promote awareness of the importance of good mental health, raise awareness of mental health disorders, provide support for mental health peers and caregivers, promote mental health literacy and support other bodies in all areas to promote mental health. MIASA thrives on peer empowerment by promoting awareness, advocacy, relief support and livelihood support. Below is MIASA's objective:

The objective of MIASA is to promote awareness on the importance of mental health, to address and clarify misconceptions on mental health issues and conditions while simultaneously providing support for peers and caregivers through its various programmes and support initiatives. Being peer-initiated, MIASA has a strong foundation and also purpose. It offers a holistic solution, not only from the medical perspective but of spirituality being a key component, highlighting the critical importance of the recovery model focusing on empowerment, autonomy and right-based approach.

I've always been searching for people who have gone through what I've experienced. For years, not knowing that there are others out there who share the same story as I do, it was such a relief to learn about MIASA. It gave me hope. There were members of MIASA whom I met, and they helped me with my emotional and mental support. There was this one friend from MIASA who had Mixed Panic Disorder and Major Depressive Disorder. She battled with her mental illness for years. There was a period in her life when she kept fainting after every panic attack. Her struggles instilled hope and faith within me. Her stories inspired me to keep fighting. I honestly think she is a true warrior because imagine fainting nearly every day, throwing up every day, gasping for air every day, facing a tsunami of negative thoughts every day, experiencing sleepless nights, and dealing with insomnia. She went through them all and survived. *Alḥamdulillāh*. She is a warrior.

There was another story about this friend of mine who was diagnosed with Borderline Disorder and Major Depressive Disorder. She was also a kind and helpful friend. Regardless of their fights, they were willing to help people in need too. They became people who listen and guide us to find a solution to our problems, and that is just so kind of them. I wish nothing but for Allah (s.w.t.) to build them a house in paradise. This shows that people with mental conditions are not weak. In fact, they are strong. Imagine fighting for yourself and then helping other people struggling in their battles. This is just so cool and insanely strong. These people are such an inspiration. Thank you for teaching me how to be strong and to keep holding on. Being within this community makes me feel less anxious and more confident with myself.

I'm thankful for their presence in my life. They are great support systems, my teachers, and the reason for me to keep trying and not give up. Sometimes, as an anxiety disorder patient like me, all I need is a person who is willing to lend an ear and a heart that can empathise without making me feel judged or criticised. For that, I thank them.

7. FIND A TRUSTED ONE

My life has always been a roller coaster ride. There were always unexpected problems and ugly surprises during the early days of my twenties. My friends told me that I was strong for facing all sorts of life problems, and I believed them. So, I endured and struggled alone, thinking I was strong enough to face everything. I was strong, but I forgot to have a support system that would always care, support, and be there for me. Someone who truly understands me. I was being so hard on myself. I was unkind to myself. And I do regret that. If only I could have been a little gentler with the younger me, things might have been different. But it's OK; this was the journey that I had to walk, and for sure Allah (s.w.t.) knows what's best for us. I want you all to know that there is no shame or wrong in reaching out for help. There is no guilt in finding the right people to share your problems with. Sometimes life can be too much for us, and we need someone to hold on to. That person could be a kind family member, a sincere friend, or any trusted person.

8. START FROM THE LITTLE STEPS TO STRENGTHEN BONDS WITH ALLAH (S.W.T.)

When people see that mending their relationship with God is something huge and big to be done, allow me to tell you that all you need are just little steps and small acts to start in order to strengthen your bond with Allah (s.w.t.). It all starts from the little good doings to rekindle that flame of yours and drive you forward to reach a better and stronger relationship. A small act of kindness is where you will find the biggest feeling of sincerity. So don't underestimate the little steps because it does really give a big meaning. It gives a big impact.

I know we all have our own personal ways to get closer to Allah (s.w.t.). The experience of each individual is different. Even the ways to get closer to God differ. But here are some of the things I do to strengthen the bond between me and God.

a. I keep a journal where I write to Allah (s.w.t.). It's a personal journal where I write love letters to God. It is where I talk about the things that happen in a day to God, from sad to happy things. This way somehow makes me feel that Allah (s.w.t.) is near and He is always there for me.

b. I read books. Ones that connect to the soul and remind me of Allah (s.w.t.). As for this, I prefer a light reading where people tell stories of how they bring themselves closer to Allah (s.w.t.) as it always offers me warmth and comfort while welcoming me back to my centre and origin.

c. Practice *dhikr*, as it is almost effortless because you can do it in your heart. And every '*astaghfirullāh*' can bring your heart closer to Allah (s.w.t.). Every '*alḥamdulillāh*' can make your soul find peace. Every '*Allāhu Akbar*' can allow your spirit to uplift. And every '*subḥanAllāh*' can give you peace.

Thus, sometimes we don't have to look far for the big ways to connect to God because there are always small little things around us that could give us great workable ways and answers. May you find your best way in getting to attain God's love and happily ever after.

In conclusion, I've shared my struggling moments of darkness and how I personally walked through them. I would like to relate such experiences to nature's phenomenon of dusk to dawn, which refers to the transition from darkness to light.

While the phrase 'dusk till dawn' can have different meanings, in this context, what I would like to portray about this phrase is the metaphor behind it. Every morning, the sun has to fight with the dark to shine in the sky, much like the idea that after hardship, there comes ease. This metaphor illustrates our great efforts in going through and surviving darkness. No matter how many hardships come our way, no matter how bad the circumstances, we should continue to have hope and faith to witness the light at dawn.

Dear you,

I would like to congratulate you for your courage to persist in finding yourself in the chaos and to find the answers to the big questions in life. It is indeed a tough journey but you were able to make it through and found you. There's a burst of inspiration in finding the wisdom within the chaos that surrounds you. There's endless beauty in accepting your insecurities & embracing your flaws. There's real empowerment in knowing your fears, admitting your mistakes & learning from your past.

There's magic in allowing your emotions and feelings in you, in being courageous to uncertainty and in being able to face doubts. Because when you show appreciation to your heart and soul, when you are OK with being who you really are, when you feel that you don't need to attain perfection for people, when you are gentle with yourself, a weight is lifted off of your shoulders and you are allowed to experience true growth to its fullest.

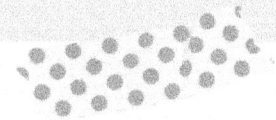

And now look in front of you. The road is still long. The journey has not yet ended. The sun has not yet set. The adventures have not yet ceased. Go on and continue walking. Go on and continue exploring. Go on and continue roaming. Go on and continue discovering. Go on and continue wandering. Time has not yet finished. There is still time for you to embark on new roads and paths. Make use of all the time given before it's taken away. Allow yourself to step into new worlds and reflect on the wonders around you. Be enlightened, be awaken and be alive.

Yours truly,

Sharifah Nadirah

On Love

You travelled through the miraculous signs

And grew into a rare gem that's marvellously shines

Whose glow and light blind the eyes

And whose heart led by wisdom and divine guides

THE PASSIONATE MUSLIM

Do what you love

The thing about the old me was that I was always insecure, unconfident, and self-conscious. I always sought approval, and because of that, I became afraid of people rejecting who I truly was and what I really loved to do. To make it safe, I made my choices based on people's preferences, popular opinions, beliefs, and ideas. I believed that their acceptance would save me from discrimination and help me survive, so I kept working on meeting people's expectations. I believed that their ideas needed to be pursued because that would make me one of them too. I wanted to be accepted and be part of them. So, I started to learn to love their ideas.

I realised that the people around us, with whom we live and grow, could really have a big impact and influence us in our lives in terms of our choices, ideas, and beliefs. But regardless of all that, I also realised that it's never too late to find ourselves, to discover our dreams, follow our passion, and take responsibility to learn our heart's melody. Break free and embark on your own journey. You don't have to be one of them. You just have to be yourself and create your own definition of success that will make you feel fuller and more alive.

I was always the girl whose heart loved to write. I was always that girl who loved to play with words. I was always that girl who got all giddy and super excited about publishing her writing and creating peaceful worlds. In the past, I always thought of letting writing be just a hobby of mine because I was not sure if I wanted to make it a career. But now, writing has become the reason for a hopeful and joyful day. It helped me grow wings, expanded my horizons, and gave me the true meaning of life.

And I know I did the right thing when I look back at my writing journey and see how far I've come (and also think and imagine that I could have probably written or published more books and could achieve more if I had chosen to be more focused on being an author earlier). But I know Allah (s.w.t.) knows best, and there will always be things that I've learned from the journey.

This journey of mine all started when I first wrote for an Islamic website, ILUVISLAM, and published a few articles there. I then self-published two books when I was in my early twenties. My first book was self-published when I was 22 years old. Next, I wrote ten e-books and self-published another book. In the end, I finally managed to traditionally publish two books in 2022: *Invoke* which had made its way across the country and was appreciated by people of many races, and *Healing the Heart* which had become a bestseller during the Kuala Lumpur International Book Fair and had made its way to number 1 in the MPH bestselling chart. What's more important is that they are loved by warm souls out there. (I truly appreciate the support.) Currently, I am very excited to have upcoming books to be published and am receiving local and international book deals. *Alḥamdulillāh ʿalā kulli ḥāl.*

This is my true passion. I want to focus on this one thing so that I am capable of thriving, growing, and flourishing. This is where I want to explore. I want to write for another thousand years, sharing stories and growing old happily.

Guys, you do you. Don't try to be someone else. Find your voice, discover your dreams, be different, and make a difference!

PS: It doesn't matter what your true dreams are and what you're passionate about doing. Even if you truly love postgraduate studies and being in the health science field is what gives you joy, then go for it. Go for what makes your soul alive and makes you excited to live for another day.

Pleasure in the job puts perfection in the work.

(Aristotle)

Nurturing Passion

Passion is the safe haven for emotions, desires, and emotional stability. It is the fundamental tool for awakening the human soul. I love to talk and write about passion, as it gives me true meaning and genuine fulfilment in life. I feel grounded, mindful, enlivened, awakened, and purposeful when my actions are guided by passionate intention. It gives me high-spirited energy to accelerate and drive forward in life. When we are engaged in an activity that brings warmth and love, we feel fuelled, thrive, and feel motivated. In psychology, this is said to be a 'flow state'. You might have felt this when you're immersed in a fulfilling activity such as painting, writing, playing a musical instrument, or reading an interesting book, without noticing time had passed. If you have ever experienced such a state, know that is what passion means—where you can glow. On a fundamental level, passion is putting your heart, mind, body, and soul into something. Passion is doing what makes you joyful and content. Here are excerpts on passion from an academic journal titled *'The role of passion in sustainable psychological well-being'*.

> *"Being passionate toward a given activity will lead the person to engage in the activity frequently, often over several years and sometimes a lifetime. Harmonious passion for a given activity will generally lead to the experience of positive emotions during activity engagement. Such emotions, in turn, will foster increases in psychological well-being. Thus, over time, harmonious passion is expected to facilitate sustainable increases in psychological well-being and prevent against ill-being."*

"Furthermore, research on passion has systematically found that regularly engaging in a meaningful activity out of harmonious passion leads to the experience of positive affect and the protection against negative affect."

I have found the magic of being led by the burning fire of the heart, and I always felt a deeper resonance when it comes to always being passionate about what can make me go through the day without feeling lost and confused. Due to that, I discovered that being a Muslim is indeed a blessing because we are always encouraged to do things with the heart, which makes us bloom magnificently to celebrate and reap the outcome of our deeds. Of all things that we will carry out in our daily life, they are started with intention, duʿaʾ, and actions of integrity that are aligned with it, showing that Islamic teaching has provided a comprehensive guide towards breeding sincerity and passion in one's heart to execute something wholeheartedly. Isn't it beautiful to do good things that benefit you and the people around you with all your heart—when all boils down to the noble *niyyah*, which is our actions and purpose in doing anything in the name of Allah (s.w.t.) including our passionate creative activities related to arts, literature, sciences, advocacy, activism? As a passionate Muslim who is aware of the relation to our state of being, our human *fitrah*, and conscience are connected to Allah (s.w.t.), we acknowledge that everything we do is for Allah (s.w.t.) whether it's uttered or not because we know that is our life motto and it serves as a constant reminder that Allah (s.w.t.) is the Lord of the worlds. It is said in the Qurʾan that:

> *Say, "Indeed, my prayer, my rites of sacrifice, my living and my dying are for Allah, Lord of the worlds.*
>
> (*surah* al-Anʿam, 6:162)

What I personally reflect on this *ayah* is that acknowledging that can help us get a better grasp of what it means to live a passionate life as a Muslim, which is to not separate the passion for the love towards your creative interest and the love of your persuasion of Allah (s.w.t.) as both can be beautifully reunited. For example, you write on success and never forget the importance of success as a Muslim in this world and the hereafter, and you draw or paint with a pure intention to bring awareness, you write so you could express your feelings and remove yourself from self-harm, you paint and sketch so you can find meaning as a human, find yourself and enjoy. Having passion for His sake is to be able to allow you to elevate your human qualities and spend time pleasing Allah (s.w.t.) and not the people, embodying that in the state of worship you strive. You are now a person with a purpose, viewing the world through a new lens. You have a mission to live, do, and speak exclusively for His sake. Having a clear purpose, vision, and mission can transform one's outlook on the world. This *dunya* becomes a source of opportunities and a repository of wealth (in the form of good deeds) for the afterlife. A passionate Muslim is also someone who values righteous deeds and does his best to be kind to others without expecting anything in return. According to the Prophet (s.a.w.):

> *…being content with what God has given you will lead to prosperity. Love others as you love yourself, and you will be a true Muslim.*
>
> (Sunan Ibn Majah 4217)

Every trial we face in this world is an opportunity to be patient and content. Every blessing they receive and witness around them serves as an opportunity for gratitude and humility. Those who resist temptation recognise it as a deceptive and enslaving force. You see, they strive to keep the *dunya* in their hands rather than their hearts. They have a mission and understand the *amanah* they are carrying because they are now living for His sake. Due to that, a believer who passionately practises his faith will feel responsible for the state of the community. The degree of our sacrifice for the perfection of our faith in this fleeting world will determine our level of accomplishment to the divine reunion in the hereafter. Your passion needs to be nurtured a little bit every day, just like a plant needs water, to the point where it becomes apparent to you and the rest of the world, enabling you to share your passion with others. Giving benefit to others with that passion of yours is one of the best ways to receive the water it needs to bloom. Thus, rather than considering what we might gain in return, we should consider how we can serve others and dedicate ourselves to the cause of Islam.

When we go back to the Prophet's (s.a.w.) time and we could see how the Prophet (s.a.w.) appreciated and cultivated the various characteristics and talents of individuals within his *ummah*. For example, we can read on Bilal (r.a.) being the *mu'adhdhin*; Umar (r.a.) for his stalwart character against the opposition of the Prophet (s.a.w.); Abu Bakr (r.a.) was a compassionate and companionable man who also excelled as a leader; 'Aʾishah (r.a.) was a scholarly and enthusiastic youth. Khadijah (r.a.) was wise, dignified, and intuitive; Nusaybah bint Kaʿb (r.a.) was a warrior; and Abu Hurayrah (r.a.) was a collector of hadith who also enjoyed cats and Ibn ʿAbbas (r.a.) was an outstanding scholar. Thus with the existence of the diversity of passionate talents and skills present in the Islamic community can be the benefit for *daʿwah*. The people of those around the Prophet (s.a.w.) reveal a rich tapestry of individuality woven together by the common fibre of Islam.

It is ignorant to think that the ideal Muslim society is one in which individuality is muted, and that the more alike we function, the better. The ideal Muslim society should be one in which we unite to pray, live Islam as a way of life, respect differences, and appreciate and encourage individual talents and personalities to flourish. We should all strive to be contribution-oriented and not demand-oriented. Therefore, we must think how we can be of service to others and how we can dedicate ourselves in the service of Islam; not of what we can get in return. The degree of our sacrifice for the perfection of our faith in this fleeting world will determine our level of accomplishment to the divine reunion in the hereafter. No work of ours can be blessed without the benefit of our prayers as from there it showed that being a passionate Muslim can lead you to the embodiment of other passion so your passion will follow. You may be passionate about writing and pursuing your dreams to become an author while carrying out *daʿwah*—writing about the beauty of Islam as writing itself is a powerful way in inspiring people and spreading good deeds. Besides that, being an artist such as painters, photographers, illustrators, and creators can depict the beauty of Allah's creation to mankind. Designers of clothing lines who have created beautiful, elegant, stylish, modest abayas do contribute to the beauty of modesty which has been taught in Islam. Hence, I pray to Allah (s.w.t.) that each and one of us will discover our passion and for the benefit of Islam and the *ummah*, while having a passion and pursuing it is a source of joy that connects us to the door of goodness in Islam. Prophet Muhammad (s.a.w.) said:

> *There are many doors to goodness. [Saying] 'Glory to God,' 'Praise be to God,' 'There is no deity but God,' enjoining good, forbidding evil, removing harm from the road, listening to the deaf (until you understand them), leading the blind, guiding one to the object of his need, hurrying with the strength of one's legs to one in sorrow*

who is asking for help, and supporting the weak with the strength of one's arms—all of these are [forms of] charity prescribed for you.

(Prophet Muhammad, Fiqh Al-Sunnah, Volume 3, Number 98)

Passion and the Reality of the Working Life

One aspect of our existence outside work is life, which is one of the aspects that many of us don't have the time to enjoy due to responsibilities and commitments. Is it difficult to find time to accomplish the things you actually love in today's busy world? Certainly, it is possible. But no one who is serious about it ever claims that following their passion is simple. But they do, however, mention that the effort was worthwhile. The truth is, while some people are fortunate enough to have their passion naturally fit into their daily lives and career, unfortunately, it doesn't always happen to everyone. They say that too many people only work for money, and what's wrong with that? In today's world, it is really difficult if we don't work for money. Working for money is a way to survive. Not all of us are fortunate enough to be given a chance to work for what we love, and not all of us too have had the opportunity yet to discover our dreams and passion. But still, there is no wrong in working for money as long as we see money as a tool rather than a destination because a paycheck is also necessary since there are taxes and bills that need to be paid. The house rent needs to be paid. The car needs to be paid for. There are loved ones that need to be fed. The family and children's basic needs, to education fees, leaving many people out there to work for money.

The cost of living is really high nowadays. It suffocates people, thus having a job regardless of whether you love it or not becomes essential to surviving. Due to this, the thing that we would always hear and learn from working people is that having fun is only possible when the weekend arrives. Having fun should only happen on the weekends when people could have their leisure time, from sleeping at home 24/7 after a whole week of labour (which some people find fun too—I guess), to visiting spas and having a trip with their family during their time off. And work would always just be work, which is something that you just need to get through until your office or work hours end, not something to have a deep connection with. This situation right here is said by Beverly D. Flaxington, an adjunct professor at Suffolk University and an expert in human behaviour, where the idea and foundation upon which the retirement industry is built is when you are finally able to stop working hard and saving a lot of money, you will be able to relax and enjoy the results of your hard work. Performing pilgrimage, overseas holiday trips, and spending time with the grandchildren come to mind. This is where we are taught that in retirement, a lifetime of work can finally end in peace, but what if you could discover happiness and fulfilment long before the moment of your retirement?

There are possible chances for you to discover what you love. It is said by Beverly D. Flaxington that many people are in a difficult position because they can't risk losing their pay check because it keeps the lights on and provides for their families. But what if, you could like what you are doing right now? What if you could bring your passion to work and create a fresh direction? Even if you are unable to leave what you are doing right now, there are ways to find fulfilment. Maybe instead of dragging yourself to wherever you need to be tomorrow, you might take a different attitude and start kindling your passion if you feel that your work life is lacking that sense of *joie de vivre*. There is a reading I did on science in applied psychology on the University of Southern California website, and it was said according to a renowned Hungarian psychologist, Mihaly Csikszentmihalyi, being able to enjoy your work is the prime element or key to entering a state of 'flow'. The meaning of 'flow' over here is the experience you're going through when you're in 'the situation/zone'. It is said that you should feel fully focused, creative, and have ideas flowing freely.

Here are some of the points by Mihaly Csikszentmihalyi :

1. Every time we are assigned a task and have a negative attitude toward it, it becomes more difficult for us to finish the assignment. Working on a project you enjoy is stimulating and stimulates a productive feedback loop. In turn, your enthusiasm for your task energises you, giving you additional drive for achievement. The secret is learning how to make yourself enjoy your work, even the most boring or difficult projects.

2. Once you take on a task with a positive mindset and think of the benefits you can reap from completing this project, your work is more likely to happen in a steady, concentrated flow. Being in this state of mind means you will be highly focused and fully absorbed in the task at hand, just as you would be while doing something you really enjoy. Being able to fully devote

yourself to a task and give it your all will make you more productive and knowledgeable, leading you towards success at work.

3. When you approach a task with a good outlook and consider the advantages you will experience upon finishing it, your work is more likely to proceed in a continuous, focused flow. You will be intensely concentrated and totally immersed in the activity at hand when you are in this frame of mind, just as you would be when doing something you really enjoy. Your ability to fully commit to a task and give it your all will increase your productivity and knowledge, which will help you succeed at work.

4. Passion not only encourages enjoyment of your work but also aids in conquering challenges at work. Remember the benefits of the work you are doing whenever you have a setback or start to question your skills. This perseverance will result in high-calibre work that elevates you and moves you one step closer to your next objective. Use that motivation and determination as fuel as you approach the next success marker.

5. Having a positive attitude and enjoying your work can increase productivity and improve results. The likelihood of being upbeat, motivated, learning more quickly, making fewer mistakes, and making better business judgements are all higher in those who enjoy their professions.

However, it is said by Dr. Sherrie Bourg Carter, Psy.D., who is a psychologist and an author who specialises in the area of women and stress, it's not as simple or as straightforward to follow your passion as how others would have you believe. Yes, stories about once-in-a-lifetime opportunities for people to pursue what they love have been told to all of us. However, rather than being the norm, this is a rare exception. For the majority of people, finding time in their schedules to pursue their passions requires perseverance, hard effort, and patience.

In a nutshell, a working life based on passion is joyful, rewarding, fulfilling as well as offering you upcoming exciting days, but you should also learn that not everybody is able to live the life of their dreams, so be kind, have empathy, offer a helping hand if you could and make *du'a'* to Allah (s.w.t.) that they will also experience the feeling of love and joy in their working hours. For the people who persevere to work with the absence of love and passion but with the presence of force and pressure, do know that there are many alternative ways to allow yourself to feel fun at work even though it might be challenging. Seeking even the slightest joy within the tough and hardest days in your life to reward yourself would mean a lot to your soul. It could miraculously revive your heart.

I know we are all struggling—even people of passion that admit they had fun at work—have struggles and I pray to Allah (s.w.t.) that He will lead you to the road that is right. May He grant you a sunny path that will lead you to brighter days. Above all suggested ways and methods to attain peace and meet our own perfect pace is to pray to Allah (s.w.t.) for grace. He would be kind enough to provide a way after effort has been made. Do know that ***WE WILL OFTEN GET LOST*** before we would find our way out. I got lost in many unclear foggy roads and got thrown to many pit stops along the way before I truly embraced my true form, my nature, my habitat, my home and my passion. It really took all of me to reach my place of love. But I felt that I will one day find a place where I could feel belonged and never give up on searching, even though the road is long but the final destination was not wrong, it was truly right all along. So remember to make an effort, seek God and make *du'a'* and always know that you are able to choose.

> *So where are you going?*
>
> (*surah* at-Takwir, 81:26)

This is one of my favourite verses in the Qur'an. It's an all-time favourite. This verse is indeed so beautiful, it possessed a real deep message. This *ayah* really hits me hard. It hits me really deep. The Holy Qur'an is a grand entranceway to the depths of the domain of contemplation and a huge vista of meditation for sincere believers. It is the heavenly and terrestrial languages. It is an inexhaustible source of inspiration and a gift of human eloquence because of the words of knowledge it offers, the food for the spirit. What I've read, learned, personally reflected and contemplated from the verse is that Allah (s.w.t.) uses a metaphor by comparing a person's choices and way of life to a physical path that one goes on and eventually leads to a destination. It's like Allah (s.w.t.) is asking them which way are you going to go right now? You can see that Allah (s.w.t.) is posing a question there.

ON LOVE

According to Imam Suyuti in his book *al-Itqan*, there are 36 different ways to understand a question that Allah (s.w.t.) poses in the Qur'an. Allah (s.w.t.) may pose a rhetorical question or one that is meant to chastise someone. This verse makes use of it to show *ta'jiz* that they are unable to answer or refute. Allah (s.w.t.) thus affirms the veracity of this Qur'an by stating that it is only a reminder after awakening them from their tasks.

Even God allows you to choose, so choose wisely.

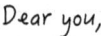

Dear you,

On the days when your heart feels that healing is extremely tiring, exhausting, and disappointing, you feel the struggles are growing stronger while your strength is turning weaker, and hope is wilting in the face of fear as doubts rise, while to courage you frantically adhere as you push yourself through the darkness, storm, and thunder. You feel cold, confused, afraid, lost, lonely, and unsure of everything. Your paths are twisted, and you worry that you are not actually progressing towards recovery. You are afraid that you have failed. You are anxious that all your efforts were meant for nothing. But that is not all true because healing is not all straight, definite, absolute, and linear. It will always make you feel that you are between black and white, and at most times you are inclined towards either. It is a process of ups and downs in order to make progress. Healing can be painful and scarring. It can be disheartening and chaotic.

It can be heartbreaking and wrenching. But somehow, healing also contained moments when you felt relieved and hopeful again, as if you were all faithful and found that healing was working for you in all its magical and miraculous ways, like everything was OK once more. Your energy was refuelled. Your spirit was ignited. Your mind and heart feel lighter, and your soul is fired up to accelerate. And when you experience these passionate, heart-warming days—the days where you are allowed to breathe, where the stars start to twinkle, where the moon glows, and where the sun shines—you will eventually realise the presence of beautiful souls that are there for you, loyally supporting, caring, loving, appreciating, and caring for you. You will feel as though you are at the end of your healing journey. And these are the precious moments that you need to treasure, place your dreams in, hold tightly to, remember, and strive for. These are the gifted moments that will guide you in finding your way to seeing the light.

Yours truly,

Sharifah Nadirah

*There are days when
your lungs hungers for air,
your body screams for care,
as your mind continues to compare
of whose temporary beauty
the crowd is aware.
Sigh, it was a snare.*

*You desire hunger for worldly pleasure,
you yearn for sparkling treasure.*

*Drawn into the ultimate deceit,
of chasing fame, recognition, wealth, status,
flaunting temporary beauty in the continuity
of debts and loans as your heart grows in worry.*

*While your heart plead for light,
your soul prayed for might.*

KNOWING THYSELF

Love Yourself

I could still remember the younger version of me who had perceived the idea of self-love wrongly and executed the self-love project in a way that had aided in the process of deteriorating my mental health. It took me many years to finally understand and grasp the true concept of self-love.

It was in my early twenties when I started to be exposed to the self-love idea promoted by the mainstream media. Which mostly teaches you to go for a makeover and work on every physical part of you from top to the toe. The typical idea encourages you to only focus on what appears on the outside rather than also working on the inside part of you or to be fair, working on both parts, in and out, hand in hand because there's no harm and wrong to be pretty girls as long as you don't ignore your inner beauty as it also needs real nurturing and care. But the old me at that time only bought the idea that it is solely important to beautify your outer glow, so being a young girl that was clueless and constantly emotionally unstable, I started to work on purchasing great skincare products, high-end makeups, learned how to wear make-ups, followed the latest fashion trend where I would always find myself stressing out to match every piece of clothing perfectly to get the perfect outfit. I also spent most of my time doing facials at spas as it helped to unwind me. I did find ease and I'm not lying about that, but it was temporary, it only kept me at ease during the moment. But after that, I felt cold, empty, distressed and alone again. I never found contentment and I always felt unfulfilled and wanted more. The more I worked on beautifying my physical aspect, the more I compared myself with other girls on social media finding myself not enough. I felt that I needed to do more and I took more selfies to prove that I appeared much better and cooler which had been pretty unhealthy due to the intention behind the action.

This unhealthy activity took a toll on my mental health. One day, I realised that what I'd been doing all this while was not to cure myself but instead it is to worsen my condition. I finally realised that I never truly embarked on the journey of self-love but I was just lost while being in painful episodes where I pursued to seek constant validation, attention and approval from the people around me. It was indeed tiring, energy consuming and not worth it. I honestly felt like slapping the old me. And to the young girls and women out there I would really want all of you to know what it really means to love yourself and what are the real ways of loving and caring for yourself so you will not end up hurting yourself even more. So allow me to share a little bit on what I've learned about the true meaning of self-love and how to carry out the acts of self-love.

'Love yourself', 'Self-care' and 'Self-love'; nearly every day we hear these words on our social media, from TikTok to Instagram but what actually comes to mind when we talk about self-love or self-care?

Self-love nowadays has become a pop culture, especially among girls or women who have been heartbroken. The idea of 'self-love' itself is usually portrayed by the mainstream media with concepts that are focused on exterior matters. Luxurious bubble baths with expensive bath bombs, facials, manicures and pedicures at renowned salons are things you must do to 'self-care'. And the list goes on up to a point where we think that we ought to be filthy rich in order to pamper ourselves and execute the self-love project itself. How much do self-love and self-care cost? Is it indeed expensive? Do we need to be among the privileged to carry out self-love?

What do self-love and self-care actually mean?

Honestly, for me, I think you need a more substantial purpose to love yourself. And the purpose is not only to make you feel good, feel beautiful or feel better than someone else, but it should be more than all of that. It should be for a more vital reason to carry out self-love and self-care so you would choose to appreciate yourself and love yourself longer. To love yourself wholeheartedly for a lifetime. It takes more than putting on great clothes and plenty of pricey makeup to declare that you love yourself. There are a lot of well-groomed folks out there who have no idea how it is to love oneself. It is heart-wrenching to know that there are people out there battling external struggles like obtaining love, success, or happiness while claiming to embrace self-love without realising its true meaning and why we really need to love ourselves—which is the foundation from which everything grows. Hence, it is crucial for us to understand why we must value ourselves. To truly love oneself, we must understand the intention, purpose, and true meaning of our actions.

That being said, let us first revisit the true meaning of self-love. First of all, bear in mind that the real concept of self-love in Islam may not be fully the same as mainstream media's definition of self-love. In Islam, the concept and meaning of self-love is something deeper, something that helps the soul as well as the outward self. Many Muslims misinterpret the concept of self-love as being egotistical, overly self-absorbed, and narcissistic. You must understand that you aren't doing self-love well if it makes you feel conceited or proud. Aspects of self-love include instilling a sense of self-worth, honouring the physical form, intellectual, and spiritual blessings Allah (s.w.t.) has bestowed upon us and taking the time to feel at ease with who you are.

The phrase "self-love" refers to a variety of loving behaviours we engage in both physically and emotionally toward ourselves. Because when you love yourself, others don't have to cope with your unresolved issues. Loving oneself is not an act of selfishness; rather, it is an act of generosity for others. Self-care entails taking care of your physical, mental, emotional, and spiritual needs. It is a significant obligation because God has given us life as a responsibility. In the end, Islamic self-love is expanding under the influence of Divine guidance. Just as studying nature and cosmology brings us closer to God, thinking about who we are, how we were made, and the wonders we possess takes us to the great Creator. We eventually come to God as we reflect on the indications we are experiencing and try to comprehend who we are. The more you grow and strive to become a better version of yourself, the more you will grow to become closer to God's light. You have the remedy to treat yourself by being aware of your own flaws, inadequacies, and shortcomings. The answer lies within you, and you are your own best physician. God will shower His blessings on you when you take the time to change to a better version of yourself and work on your heart to be more sincere, and honest and remove the inner impurities.

One of the reasons is the beloved messenger of Allah (s.w.t.), Prophet Muhammad (s.a.w.) was sent to this world for the purpose to teach mankind how to love themselves the right way and create ideal, healthy selves. This was done by him (s.a.w.) guiding us all to the path that helps us recognise the circumstances that lead to the onset of self-neglect. He shared knowledge about how to look after ourselves, how to have confidence in ourselves, and how to be able to admit and deal with one's flaws.

Here are personal ways that I adopted to practise self-love:

1. EMBARKING ON SELF-EXPLORATION

According to the Prophet (s.a.w.), Allah (s.w.t.) is beautiful and He appreciates beauty. Allah (s.w.t.) creates beauty in every creation of His so there is indeed something beautiful in you that is ought to be discovered. There is indeed something beautiful in you that you must love. Spend some time reflecting on your life by connecting with yourself.

Investing time and energy to explore yourself in improving your knowledge of yourself is always worthwhile. Take a break from doom-scrolling through social media and take some time to connect with yourself and your heart and reflect on your life. Learn and read on self-healing and self- growth as reading gives us a window onto an array of unexplored worlds. It is said by Aristotle:

Knowing yourself is the beginning of all wisdom.

To read and learn, teaches us lessons and broadens our knowledge by guiding our brain's development and learning. You can learn and read on how to heal from your past pain, and trauma while embarking on a spiritual journey in finding God and exploring your true path in the different aspects in life. You can learn how to deal with difficult emotions, and knowing your best qualities, your strengths and accomplishments, and the things that you love in life that can lead you to a well-experienced life. Keep in mind that loving who you are and what you do every day is crucial to your journey of self-development and exploration. What's even better is if you start writing yourself a love letter to express the things you love about yourself. It can be challenging to find the things you love about yourself as we are all experts at identifying every single thing that we hate about ourselves. But maybe you can ask a close friend or loved one on what qualities they value most about you. Understanding what others think of you can help you recognise those qualities within yourself. Knowing our strengths allows us to take advantage of them, use them to improve ourselves, the lives of those around us, and become closer to Allah (s.w.t.) and His mercy.

Next is to acknowledge the flaws and shortcomings of ourselves as well as the limitations we have in the conditions of our lives, and as we go through all of this it actually brings our focus back to the existence of the ultimate Creator. By studying ourselves, our abilities, the way our bodies and mind work, and the way we are shaped and designed, we can comprehend the fact of the need to depend on the Almighty creator, where we accept our vulnerability as imperfect humans. And knowing our shortcomings and understanding our weaknesses can help us to improve them and brings us closer to Allah (s.w.t.) and keeps us from committing sins. It becomes increasingly clear as we gain a deep awareness of our strengths and weaknesses that we have the wisdom behind the existence of everything that exists within us. We are directed to a Higher, Supreme Being whose existence is unquestionable by all signs that are embedded in both ourselves and the world around us. Thus, invest in self-exploration that brings self-knowledge. The more knowledge we possess, the greater our fear of Allah (s.w.t.), according to Abu Bakr (r.a.).

As I mentioned before there is a classic Arabic proverb:

Whosoever knows himself knows his Lord.

This proverb implies that gaining knowledge about oneself leads to knowledge about Allah (s.w.t.). Undoubtedly, the longest relationship you'll ever have in life is with yourself. Invest on yourself. You can improve the many aspects of yourself when you dedicate yourself to self-exploration. You will discover your ability to manage emotions, relationships, your job, and the ups and downs of life by investing more in yourself. Even though self-discovery isn't always easy or enjoyable, the sense of fulfilment and inner peace you experience as a result of working towards your best self makes the effort worthwhile. True contentment lies in gaining knowledge to enlighten our minds and hearts, and the most beneficial form of knowledge comes from knowing oneself.

2. ENGAGING IN TAFAKKUR

It is said by 'Umar al-Khattab (r.a.):

You should have some proportion of solitude or else you will become heedless.

One of the most precious gifts that God has given us is our ability for contemplation and reflection. Maybe there's something incredibly fundamental about man that makes him drawn to find answers within himself, when the world has shown itself as much as it can. Engaging in deep, thoughtful reflection and understanding will contribute to the valuable skill of spending time in deep concentration about a belief, idea, or perception. The goal is to discover an insight beyond its obvious meaning or worth. Deep self-reflection is known as *'tafakkur'*. It is a way to ponder on one's thoughts, actions and ponder over one's creation, other creation as well as their purpose in life. It is a way of realigning balance in oneself with the world, discovering oneself and reflecting on the Oneness of God, the Creator of the universe. It is mentioned in the Qur'an that:

> *Do they not contemplate within themselves? Allah has not created the heavens and the earth and what is between them except in truth and for a specified term. And indeed, many of the people, in the meeting with their Lord, are disbelievers.*
>
> (*surah* ar-Rum, 30:8)

> *Then do they not reflect upon the Qur'an? If it had been from [any] other than Allah, they would have found within it much contradiction.*
>
> (*surah* an-Nisa', 4:82)

A believer should be inspired in making efforts to seek Allah's (s.w.t.) blessings, mercy, and eternal paradise through the contemplation of the Qur'an, to reflect on the past nation stories, the miraculous signs of Allah (s.w.t.), and the divine character of the final messenger, Prophet Muhammad (s.a.w.). The Prophet (s.a.w.) holds true solid faith in Allah (s.w.t.) and submitted himself to His will. He (s.a.w.) carried out a set of morality of speech, actions and intentions represented the divine message of peace. The Prophet (s.a.w.) showed how one can reach their full potential with dedicating oneself in learning to reflect on the blessings and wisdom behind Allah's (s.w.t.) creations and how it can positively influence you.

Tafakkur or reflection can be tailor made to your own personal comfortable way. You can reflect whenever and wherever you want; you can seclude and isolate temporarily in a place free from distractions. You can use weekend nights to work on musings, thinking back on the day's events. As you reflect on yourself; have an uplifting perspective. Examine the good elements of your life before focusing on the areas where you could have performed better. Acknowledge that everything is a part of Allah's (s.w.t.) plan including the predestination and fate which are concepts shared by Muslims. Know that everything that happens is for a reason and for every event has a purpose, which we think will ultimately lead us to fulfil our mission. We were not created to live, love, or suffer pointlessly, as there is wisdom and reason that exist for every event in our lives to be interconnected for the next chapter of our life to unfold. Every person that you have crossed paths with must have a reason and as Muslims, we believe that our lives don't just happen out of randomness and coincidence. Events serve as a lesson and figuring out why this happens to you is also key to finding clarity in your life. Lastly, try to see yourself in the future if you continue in this manner at present. Keeping an eye on your behaviour and staying directed towards your goals is made possible when you visualise yourself in a realistic time frame. There are countless distractions in our daily lives. On-going reflection is necessary for our body, heart, and mind. In the cave of Hira', when the revelations started, Prophet Muhammad (s.a.w.) took some time to reflect on his feelings. This is where we can learn to recognise and accept our feelings—no matter how uncomfortable—as seen by the life of Prophet Muhammad (s.a.w.). A ninth century Muslim physician known as Abu Zayd Al-Balkhi often discussed the nature of this life and how it is a home for anxiety, trials, worry, and sadness. He also emphasised the value of self-awareness in determining what to avoid and what one's soul can withstand. Hence, self-reflection is a process of self-love and self-awareness, not just self-help. It strengthens your mental, spiritual, and mental resilience.

3. BREAKING UP WITH BAD HABITS

A habit becomes harmful to us when it crosses the boundaries from beneficial to dubious—when it interferes with our regular tasks, takes up valuable time, or jeopardises our mental, physical, or emotional health. The bad habits we are unaware of cause us more harm because we are unaware of how they affect us personally or how they affect other people. Humans are habitual beings so when bad habits are formed and established deeply in our subconscious mind, we start doing them without thinking. We lose awareness of them to the point where we might be caught off guard if a friend or loved one pointed them out to us. Some people have a habit of swearing, while others may have a habit of procrastination, lashing out anger or engaging in constant gossip. Know that these will hinder your ability to feel close to Allah (s.w.t.). Thus choose to overcome such bad habits to improve in your relationship with Him and to use it as a chance to draw nearer to Allah (s.w.t.). In order to learn how to replace unhealthy habits with healthier ones, unlearn the bad ones and learn the good ones. To do this, one must seek knowledge and awareness. We need to understand how awareness fits into the bigger picture. A certain amount of self-awareness and reflection is required to separate good habits from bad. One becomes more self-aware when they reflect. In turn, self-awareness allows the understanding of bad habits that frequently result in unhealthy patterns, and the most effective ways to replace them with healthy new habits. Instilling self-reflection and repentance will lead you through the process. Moreover, building strong willpower, setting realistic goals, and enduring gradual steps towards changes can be a way to overcome bad habits as changing bad habits is a journey that calls for dedication, contemplation, and faith in Allah's (s.w.t.) wisdom. Islam has taught us how to live a fulfilling life by empowering us to always seek knowledge, surrounding ourselves with supportive people, and working consistently. We can overcome our bad habits while striving to improve ourselves by sincerely repenting, praying, and asking Allah (s.w.t.) for forgiveness.

4. MINDING YOUR THOUGHTS

Try to figure out why you're mentally holding onto unhealthy thoughts and experiences, and what purpose they serve you. When you understand why you do what you do, it becomes easier to imagine yourself in a healthy state of mind and feeling the way you do. Make envisioning a daily practice. Make it a habit to focus solely on the healthy aspects of your daily life. Choose your thoughts with care, just as you would choose your best clothes every day. What you allow yourself to focus on determines your mental growth. Be careful what you focus on because it will consume you and manifest in various forms. Abu Zayd Al-Balkhi emphasised the importance of contemplating healthy thoughts that are unrelated to thoughts that cause mental distress. By doing so, we can train our thoughts to cultivate gratitude for our current situation while also developing the strength to avoid falling into hopelessness and defeat.

5. *SEEKING A WISE PERSON*

Al-Balkhi emphasised the importance of seeking the counsel of a wise person in the form of a discussion or counselling in order to aid with one's unhealthy thinking and actions habits or change one's thoughts and behaviours for the better. In the book *Sustenance of the Soul*, he described the importance of having a counsellor to oversee one's actions in incorporating with the internal self-treatment approach, which in this case is the healthy contemplating process mentioned earlier. Having an outsider's perspective and having an advisor or friend oversee us can help us change our unfavourable habits significantly by merely allowing someone to bring them to our level of consciousness. Due to that, seeking therapy can also help us in reforming our inner selves and can increase one's quality of life and instil hope.

6. KNOWING THAT SELF-CARE IS AN 'IBADAH

Self-care focuses on nurturing the body and soul. Self-care is an *'ibadah*.

Prophet Muhammad (s.a.w.) said:

...Your body has a right over you, your eyes have a right over you and your wife has a right over you.

(Ṣaḥiḥ al-Bukhari 5199)

You must learn to evaluate strengths and needs if you don't want to perish from neglecting yourself while serving the *ummah*, the community, and our cultures. Islam places a strong focus on goodness.

The Prophet (s.a.w.) said:

There are two blessings that many people are deceived into losing: health and free time.

(Ṣaḥiḥ al-Bukhari 6412)

Abu Hurayrah (r.a.) relates that Allah's (s.w.t.) Messenger (s.a.w.) said:

Whoever alleviates a burden among the burdens of the world for his brother, Allah alleviates a burden among the burdens of the Day of Judgement for him. And whoever covers (the faults) of a Muslim, Allah covers him in the world and in the Hereafter. And whoever makes things easy for one in dire straits, Allah makes things easy for him in the world and the Hereafter. Allah is helping as long as the (His) Slave is helping his brother...

(Jamiʿ at-Tirmidhi 2945)

However, how can we even consider upholding the rights of others if we are unable to uphold our own? How will you help your brothers and sisters if you are unable to care for yourself? In Islam, it is required to provide assistance to others. It is similar to how it is necessary for you to protect your body, which is an *amanah* from Allah (s.w.t.). These two acts of worship are intercorrelated and linked to one another. Allah's (s.w.t.) commandments are seamlessly interconnected.

You matter.

You presume you are a small entity, but within you is enfolded the entire Universe.

(Imam 'Ali bin Abi Ṭalib (r.a.))

In conclusion, let us allow ourselves to work on loving and caring for ourselves and practise self-love and self-care. Know that in Islam self-love is unselfish. But remember, you can't put yourself first while ignoring others in need. Islam instructs us to put others before ourselves. And that does not mean you must fully put aside your own needs. It works by attaining balance for both. And what's more important is that God must be the centre of attention; self-love works successfully when it is intended for God. Allow self-love to be motivated by and for God.

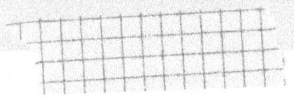

Dear you,

You don't have to always be the strongest person in the room. You can't expect yourself to constantly be strong. Nobody should expect never-ending strength from you, as though you are an unbreakable soul; as if you are strong enough to handle it all alone; as if you are the insensitive one; the one with thick skin; the one who everyone can always depend on. Please. You're human. Remember that you have feelings and emotions. You need rest, and it's not shameful to have moments of vulnerability. It's OK to be sad or scared. It's OK if you're afraid, crying, unsure, and trying to figure things out as you walk through the journey. Embracing your human nature without allowing your ego to interfere means realising you are human, and no one can blame you for that. It's OK to be human without needing the multiple masks you put on.

There will be days when you have placed your trust but then be disappointed and betrayed making your heart feel crushed and hurt. But there is nothing you can do but endure such throbbing pain with silent tears and prayers. On days when you feel the weight on your chest is about to make your heart explode, I want you to know that: You are not your pain. You are not your mistakes. You are not your failures. You are not your disappointment. You are not your doubts and fears. You are not your tears. You are not your anxiety. You are not your depression. You are not your problem. You are not your ugly thoughts. You are not your unwelcome feelings. You are not your unhealthy expectations. You are not your self-critic. You are not your past tragedy. But you're just a human who is enduring a series of tests and trials in life. May Allah (s.w.t.) ease your way and your affair and may Allah (s.w.t.) heal you.

Yours truly,

Sharifah Nadirah

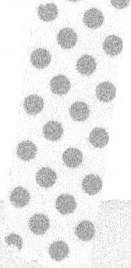

of shattered hearts,

shattered limbs their soul continues to live

of shattered spirits,

shattered minds their faith knows no limits

of shattered hope,

shattered home they go on and cope

of shattered love

shattered warmth they persist in rising above

FACING DISCRIMINATION

'Holier-than-thou'

I believe there is a reason why we are all tested differently by Allah (s.w.t.) as He knows best how much pain we can bear and how much strength we have to endure such hardship. There is wisdom behind such differences, as we are all created differently. We all have different reactions and responses to situations. So please don't compare your pain to others. You might see that your hardship is harder, and you might see that your problems are bigger, but you'll never know how the pain is testing them or how the calamities are shaking them. Don't judge them or say anything that might make them feel useless. Know that we live in a world where we tend to extend judgements quickly compared to compassion. We live in a world where we don't want to own our mistakes and are ignorant towards other people's pain. This makes people give up on each other, lose trust in one another, traumatise each other, and start to isolate themselves, wanting to be alone. People grow apart from one another because the most tiring thing is sharing your feelings only to be ignored, judged, and betrayed.

People are running and hiding from each other just so they feel safe. So please, the least we could do is not tell people that what they are going through is *nothing*. I want you all to know that bad judgements and negative treatments are the acts of injustice to another Muslim, and it brings emotional pain and mental turmoil for a person who is searching for the light or even for the ones that are not seeking. Islam is a religion that never promotes or encourages negative judgements towards one another in terms of the hardship one goes through or one's level of religiosity because Islam is filled with compassion. It does not teach the pious to look down upon anybody regardless of their hardships, character or background. Islam does not teach the fully covered person (regarding *awrah*) to dictate the partially covered or non-covered person. Islam teaches us to be human not to be a judge and a holier-than-thou individual as such behaviour drives people away from the faith.

Prophet Muhammad (s.a.w.) said in The Last Sermon:

All mankind is from Adam and Eve, an Arab has no superiority over a non-Arab nor a non-Arab has any superiority over an Arab; also a white has no superiority over a black nor a black has any superiority over white except by piety and good action.

Thus, we are all the same in Allah's (s.w.t.) sight, and what differentiates us is our sincerity in our *taqwa*. If you're a Muslim who wears a hijab, covers your *awrah* fully, prays five times a day, recites the Qur'an, learns about Islamic knowledge, listens to Islamic preachings, recites *dhikr*, performs *hajj*, engages in sunnah fasting or fasts in Ramadan, prays at the mosque, studies at an Islamic school, and participates in *usrah*, these are not reasons to look down upon the efforts of others. Our Prophet (s.a.w.) never engaged in such holier-than-thou behaviour. Islam is a compassionate religion revealed by the Most Compassionate, Allah (s.w.t.). Instead, support others;

don't belittle them. Don't hurt someone until they cry out to Allah (s.w.t.) in *sujud* at night. Avoid such actions.

Religion is not a tool to simply devilised or angelised a person; that is not the usage of religion. Islam offers much more than judgements; it was the core factors beyond judgements that allowed the Islamic civilisation during The Golden Age to preserve for centuries. Always remember we are not all truly knowledgeable and that's the reason for the first *ayah* that was revealed which is *"Iqra'"* meaning *read*. When you read, you will realise there is so much more to Islam than just feeling pious while giving judgements and causing discomfort to those who seek truth and light.

Educate, don't hate. Avoid showing hatred. Don't judge or criticise someone's life choices easily or harshly. Don't act as if you know everything because there will always be someone who knows better; you don't know everything. Remain compassionate and professional when giving statements or opinions. Respect that this world is filled with different backgrounds and upbringings

Pressures on Contemporary Muslim Women

Contemporary Muslim women refers to the groups of Muslim women who are living in the current era, originating from different walks of life and have varied values, beliefs, ideologies, worldviews, perspectives, opinions, and lifestyles. Most no longer adhere to the toxic cultural and traditional ways of living, and they refuse to be oppressed by the misconceptions of the hypocrisy of toxic extreme traditionalists in upholding patriarchal beliefs in Islam towards women. As Muslims, we must always put the teachings of the Qur'an into practice. It is mentioned in the Qur'an:

> *Take what is given freely, enjoin what is good, and turn away from the ignorant.*
>
> (*surah* al-A'raf, 7:199)

Islam does not forbid us from embracing our cultural traditions, but the certain unhealthy cultures that are toxic may be in violation of the Islamic laws. As shown by the Arab community before the coming of Prophet Muhammad (s.a.w.), some cultures and traditions must be dismissed because they are harmful to society rather than beneficial. When the rights of people are restored then only will we be able to use the best qualities of our culture and the teachings of Islam to better ourselves and our community.

Islam aims to remove bad and protect what is good in society, as how it was during the Prophet Muhammad's (s.a.w.) time. During that time, the Makkan community engaged in a number of toxic cultures that were detrimental to society, including drinking, gambling, burying daughters, and sharing wives.

The Patriarchal Muslim Men

Moreover, as for nowadays, we have the existing toxic patriarchal culture that silences women by weaponising the verses of the Qur'an to their advantage. These hypocrite, manipulative, narcissistic, and egocentric patriarchal groups had misinterpreted the teachings of Islam and used such misconceptions to confuse, pressure, and belittle women into obeying them forcefully. Women wanting to express themselves are being silenced with feel-good factors. They are told that women should just endure passively, showing patience in the face of injustice. Their partners may use Qur'anic verses to dismiss any actions women might take to liberate themselves from harm and danger to their mental health. Usually, the upbringing in families and schools in the country are not focusing on advocating and instilling the art of emotional intelligence; young women or teenagers are not taught how to regulate emotions in facing life's tribulations and would just be told by an *ustadh* or *ustadha* to just passively rely on God without any actions or effort. Such malpractice of Islamic teachings will appear perplexing to women, and some who did not go forth with sufficient Islamic knowledge will find that Islam is an oppressing religion and grow to rebel and even leave the religion.

Furthermore, with the existing religious figures that no longer adhere to morality and integrity and shamelessly execute the malpractice of polygamy, which is in many ways unaligned with Islamic teachings, justifying such an inhumane act in the name of the Prophet (s.a.w.) has created massive controversy among contemporary women. Such an act is indeed a disgrace and a *fitnah* to the Islamic community and brings misunderstandings to Islam as a whole. The tragic case of betrayal and malpractice in polygamy has also become one of the main contributors to the deterioration of women's mental health. Women are disproportionately affected by mental illnesses. In addition to the problems unique to women, such as PMDD, PMS, postpartum depression, and many others, women are more likely to experience anxiety, depression, panic attacks, and suicidal thoughts.

When women are out of balance due to mental and domestic abuse, it affects their children, causing generational trauma and pain. Children witness endless fights in the household and experience a broken family. Generational trauma often stems from toxic traditions and extreme patriarchal practices of older generations. These practices have normalised mental abuse and violence, terrifying our grandmothers and mothers to the point where they may not even realise the mental health problems they are experiencing. Continuing such a vicious cycle can lead to the collapse of future family institutions.

The truth is, women's poor mental health results from a combination of issues, including pressure from their various duties, gender discrimination, overwork, and domestic violence. Mental health issues in women are related to multifaceted factors. However, mental health issue is often seen as a taboo or a myth in the Muslim community, when in fact, the Prophet addressed such mental health problems in the Qur'an and hadith multiple times. Muslim scholars in the Golden Age of Islam built hospitals known as *maristans* or *bimaristans* that worked on a holistic approach to addressing mental health conditions. Dr. Rania Awaad, a scholar and psychiatrist, passionately relates Islam and mental health, highlighting these historical aspects.

In addition, apart from married women, single women are often pressured by the toxic conventional way of thinking that believes women need to settle by the age of thirty— being married and having children. While there are multiple reasons why women choose not to settle down early, such as facing mental illness, financial instability, and other priorities that they would want to improve and work on, women are still bound by unhealthy pressures and expectations from their community. Nevertheless, there also exists a group of judgemental Islamic women who believe they are better than others. They look down upon differences in appearance and lifestyles. These are the sisters who make harsh judgements and discriminate against people who do not cover or dress as modestly as they do, or who do not interpret Islam as literally as they do. For example, they may consider those who do not join *usrah* to be less pious or sinners who do not belong to the Islamic community. Their discourse often revolves around what is haram, without extending compassion, and they limit themselves to their own narrow definition of Islam. Some Muslim women refuse to be open to allowing Islam to reach a wider audience across races, religions, and cultures. Their lifestyles seem critical of women who do not think or appear like them. They may even practise extreme *ikhtilat* measures, where even simple interactions, including work, are not allowed.

Hence, I've been seeking answers to many questions related to 'holier-than-thou and judgemental people' in Islamic organisation movements from individuals with a wealth of experience and wisdom in Islamic community movements, including those who have retired from participating in and managing Islamic community organisations. My aspiration is to advocate against the number of existing groups that uphold toxic judgements, toxic solidarity, holier-than-thou beliefs, bias, and are less compassionate in the Islamic community.

One time, I met with my husband's *naqib*, with whom my husband had found great wisdom, comfort, and warmth in being under his guidance. I am happy for him and also aspire to have such a genuine connection within the sisterhood of Islamic community movements or organisations. I sought his opinions and perspectives on issues related to Islamic movements or organisations, including the nature of women and men in these movements, gender dynamics in business organisations, and the generation gap within Islamic organisations.

Our discussion was fruitful, gradually dispelling my confusion and leaving me feeling enlightened and relieved after receiving inspiring insights and information. Particularly interesting was his discussion on the history of Islamic movements and the ideologies of the people in these organisations, which prompted me to realise the need to read and study more on the topic. One of the key points highlighted was the importance of *akhlak,* morality, compassion, and empathy in the brotherhood and sisterhood communities.

Ultimately, I found answers to many of my questions and was able to share my thoughts and concerns. Thank you for your time and wisdom, Encik Harith Roslizar.

FACING JUDGEMENTAL PEOPLE

One of the people who really moved and inspired me was Dr. Harlina Siraj, a medical specialist, academician, speaker, author, and inspirational figure who has contributed abundantly to women's empowerment, impacting individuals and communities on a large scale. I perceive her as a symbol of female empowerment.

During a live Instagram session with Dr. Har, I found her words very resonating, drawing me deep into the conversation and discussion. She is the role model that contemporary Muslim women need in today's era when facing judgements. Below are my personal takeaways from her empowering sharing:

1. In a world of diverse beliefs and inclinations, balance is key to alignment with human nature. Strive to maintain balance, avoiding extremes that can lead you off the right track.

2. Don't be swayed by extreme groups that try to define you with their idealistic cynicism and scepticism. You are not bound by their notions, and you are beyond what they define you as.

3. You can't change anyone who doesn't want to be changed, or help anyone who doesn't want to be helped. Accept reality and be ready to deal with diversity, experience agreeing to disagree, and find common ground to connect.

4. Your aim in fighting for women's rights is not to become the opposite of your nature, but to embrace your uniqueness and celebrate your feminine power. Uncover the uniqueness in yourself and celebrate your being as a whole.

5. Understanding the difference between a growth mindset and a fixed mindset can help you acquire knowledge, wisdom, maturity, empathy and compassion.

6. A supportive community with shared values and beliefs empowers women with a vision, breeding strong, principled figures who are rooted, grounded, unbothered, and unyielding.

7. Being a visionary woman on a mission to fight against injustice means facing toxicity, negativity, judgement, scepticism, criticism, and cynicism. However, your willpower, persistence, and passion can be stronger in driving you forward to witness change.

I personally learned from and was truly inspired by passionate women who not only chased after what they loved but also protected it. I am truly inspired by women who courageously go for what they dream of, who hold on to their missions and visions. To all these women, I thank you for being the reason I keep going in life.

Dear you,

To the women who removed themselves from the toxic environment and pressure that surrounded them, and paved their own trail in building an empire out of bricks of grit, hope, love, and faith, I want you to know that you are an inspiration.

To the women who practise endless compassion and empathy but always stand up for themselves and voice out their rights to defend themselves from being used and mistreated, I want you to know that you are a kind soul with a firm spirit.

To the women who have gone through sleepless nights and emotionally testing moments in always finding a way and making efforts to go for all ways possible to earn and being financially self-dependent, who are able to cater their own spending with their own authority, I want you to know that you are powerful and amazing.

To the women who know that they are mentally ill and are not ashamed by the stigma and judgements of others and still live an incredible life; carving out their desires while seeking help and treatment, I want you to know that you are phenomenal.

To the women who have always worked on being educated and having that intelligence and intellectual capacity in you and in helping the people around you, I want you to know that you are inspiring.

To the women who strongly fight their struggles, doubts, insecurities, and feelings of inferiority in order to obtain confidence and self-esteem and thus gain victory, you are indeed empowering.

To the women who know what they want and are on the path to painting their future, thank you for being there. To the modern woman who holds on to modesty, sincerity, honesty, and loyalty in the name of her Lord, I want you to know that you are a role model.

To the women who protected their freedom of being able to be righteous women of knowledge, enlightenment, and pursuit in whatever they love and choose to do, I hope nobody will ever take away that freedom from you, as I want you to know that you are a bird to not be caged but to be flown to the clouds and reach the sky.

Dear sisters! Be alive and thrive!

Yours sincerely,

Sharifah Nadirah

*To the girl who left her island,
crossing borders, seas, and lands.*

*To the girl who went against strong currents,
violent waves, and horrendous storms.*

*To the girl who walked through forests and ruins,
wandering on unknown paths, confused roads,
and uncertain trails.*

To the girl who was trapped in the maze.

*To the girl who was drowned
in the depths of darkness,
tasted fear, and struggled with doubt.*

ON LOVE

To the girl who felt endless pain, bearing wounds and carved scars within her soul.

To the girl who pushed through the pitch-black night and marched forward with brilliance and endurance in the light of hope.

To the girl who embraced her calling and found home.

To the girl who now walks under the starry night sky, adorned with twinkling stars waving at her.

May you shine throughout life;
day and night.

On Contentment

TAKING CARE OF MENTAL HEALTH

In a world where your life choices become issues—your career choice, your study course option, your body type or size, and your skin colour or condition—all become negative issues. I suggest you don't engage with such matters; don't participate, as it will disturb your inner self and not contribute to your peace of mind. The realisation hits me that when you tell yourself that who you really are isn't OK and you pretend to be someone you are not—that's when it's time to stop. Our emotions can sometimes be overwhelming, and we may not choose what to feel when it comes to our emotions. We might try to deny the uncomfortable emotions that arise from within us, ignore them, push them away in our balloon of accumulated emotions, and refuse to experience them. But that will only make things worse. The balloon will expand and eventually explode, and we will have to face a tsunami of emotions.

Moreover, this is also due to toxic positivity, where individuals have misconceptions about the definition of true positivity, when it is most applicable, how it should be fostered, and how to effectively conduct it. While our self-confidence and sense of purpose are strengthened by positivity, positive thinking can lead to a deteriorating state of mind when used improperly. In life, we will encounter people who appear constantly positive, but they never allow their negative emotions to be healthily felt or dealt with. These people always advocate for positivity, which mostly dismisses negative emotions that also make us human, such as sadness and anxiety. They would tell you not to cry and to push away negative feelings; this is labelled as 'toxic positivity'. Toxic positivity is often forceful and persistent, and it involves avoiding, concealing, or rejecting unpleasant feelings or experiences, resulting in stress. Below are examples of toxic positivity vs healthy positivity:

Toxic Positivity:

"Be positive! Don't be sad and weak!"

Healthy Positivity:

"I am sad. I am aware of what I feel, and I am allowing myself to be human. I am allowing myself to not like this

feeling, but I am also not going to deny it; I believe that I am strong for not hiding from the pain, but instead, I am letting myself feel and experience it. I am then going to take my time and space to process what's going on, to reflect on it, learn from it, and reveal the wisdom, followed by taking appropriate healthy steps in handling the issue and reframing my unhealthy thoughts and altering the way I perceive things to let goodness and betterment take place for my mental and emotional well-being."

From positive psychology comes the birth of true and healthy positivity, where Barbara Fredrickson, a researcher in positive psychology, stated that not all positive thinking is good. Even with a positive outlook, you could still run into problems or have bad days. Instead of trying to control life, the goal is to react to it. You put your knowledge to use by cultivating virtues that not only make you feel good but also help you and those around you live longer, healthier lives with more success and fulfilling relationships. It makes life most worthwhile, although the focus of positive psychology is on strength, happiness, and fulfilment. Positive psychology does not downplay or overlook the very serious issues that people face; it does not state or imply that the issues should be abandoned or replaced. But it tackles all the areas that are needed to bring about a healthy, positive life, and identifying one's character strengths is considered a crucial aspect on the road to a good and meaningful life by positive psychology. Hence, there is a clear difference between toxic positivity that brings harm and true and healthy positivity that brings good changes in life.

I want you to know that our emotions are parts of us. All emotions and feelings are part of human nature and experience. Remember that your emotions are simply a reflection of how your life is going for you. Most of the time, people don't need to suppress their bad emotions. They must pay attention to and react to the information they are learning from those feelings. I think we should slowly learn to let them all in, to accept each and every emotion, to sit with each one, and to appreciate each one while knowing that the emotions will not stay forever. When we allow ourselves to understand our emotions, it will magically allow us to be in touch with our souls, hearts, true feelings, and inner voices, letting the emotions teach us lessons of wisdom along the way. The experience of feeling the emotions is not all about being aware of your thoughts and feelings but it is also a practice of self-acceptance. Understanding that it's often not about what occurs to you, but how you interpret these situations, can be difficult if you struggle with negative thoughts, especially when these negative thoughts become habitual. Negative thinking can lead to depressive, anxious, or negative thoughts.

Many of us struggle with mental health problems today. In a time when mental health problems will always occur in society, starting from the family to the workplace, due to the toxic and unhealthy culture and environment it provides, which is saddening, we need to be educated on the importance of prioritising our mental health. Each individual should be equipped with knowledge of mental health. Our emotional, psychological, and social well-being are all parts of our mental health. It influences our thoughts, emotions, and behaviours. Additionally, it influences how we respond to stress, interact with others, and make good decisions. Poor mental health and mental illness are not the same thing, despite the fact that the phrases are sometimes used interchangeably. Even if a person does not have a mental disorder, they can have poor mental health. Thus, here are some personal ways that have helped me in protecting my mental health:

Overcoming Your Fears

Fear is such a strong feeling. People wouldn't be able to guard themselves against real threats if they didn't experience fear. Fear is an essential emotional and physical defence mechanism that has played a crucial role in human life. It can keep us secure, but for many of us, it paralyses us and prevents us from living life to the utmost. We can shut down if our fears spiral out of control. We are vulnerable to being kept rigid by them. But we're here to live our lives properly, and if we don't face and contain our fears, they may prevent us from experiencing the joy of life. No one is immune to fear, but those who are seen as courageous may handle their anxieties in ways that serve as role models for others. Being mindful of one's thoughts, recognising one's anxieties, and being in the moment can all help one manage everyday fears. The first step is to challenge the myth that underlies fear. The capacity to take a step back, acknowledge those ideas as stories, and calmly assess whether they are accurate or rational can be a powerful start in overcoming them when one's mental projections suggest that something will go wrong or that a person faces approaching danger. But we must approach our fears rationally if we want to control them. We can sit with the understanding that if we take a certain action, we might experience a result that we don't want to happen instead of living life mindlessly. Confront the fear when you are ready, and repeat it for practice. Keep practising the principles of exposure. As humans, our fear is a natural phenomenon. So, as you go through these ups and downs, be gentle with yourself. Everybody has fear. The key is how you respond to it. It gives you power and puts you in charge of your life when you view it as a struggle that must be dealt with and create a plan for it. Examine your fears and what it would take to overcome them. You can take it in little steps depending on how comfortable you are with change. The biggest step is to start thinking about fear as baggage rather than as a necessary addition. It is your responsibility to identify the source of those unfavourable and anxious thoughts so that you can take steps to get rid of them.

Practising Self-distancing

The ability to reflect on one's own experiences from the viewpoint of an outside observer as opposed to a more inwardly focused point of view is known as "self-distancing". We frequently find ourselves in dilemmas where we are unable to grasp the bigger picture of an unwanted situation. For instance, it may be difficult to comprehend the effects of what has happened while we are under intense stress, anxiety, despair, or rage. Here is where we can use the method of psychological distance to our advantage. According to research, embracing a more realistic perspective encourages people to give bad experiences more meaning.This is probably due to the fact that people may generalise experiences when they are viewed from a distance, allowing them to concentrate on the wider picture rather than presenting elements of more delicate, negative feelings.

I know that the more we want to hold on to it, the more it makes us question our sanity. The more we feel uncomfortable with ourselves, and due to that, we decide to silence our inner voice, because it might be easier for some of us to just ignore the alarming inner voice that is screaming for help and care. I know I've been there, even though I could not fully understand, but I could relate and feel more or less the same. But here is something that I've learned: anything that robs your inner peace and brings harm to your mental health will never be worth it. And I learned it the hard way. I used to want people to like or love me without trying to like or love myself first. I learned that we can't force a person to like or love us, but we sure can try our best to allow ourselves to embrace the flaws within us, accept our own mistakes, and grow to like and love ourselves better.

Indulge in the Things that Bring You Calmness and Love

Spend time with what you love. Finding something that you find fulfilled, joyful and alive, is what you need to pursue and do. What makes you get out of bed in the morning is what you should channel your energy to. Based on my experience when you do what you love to do when you follow your passion, magic happens! Healing happens, and recovery happens! Doing what you love is therapeutic, it heals. I used to spend my day and nights writing in order to make me less anxious and in control again and it tremendously worked. I believe that if something makes your heart flutter is something worth going after.

Acknowledging the Intoxication of Comparison

Comparison is a key part of our thought process, whether it be conscious or unconscious. Examples include comparing our appearance, our fame, wealth, career and many more. If negative comparisons persist, we will be led to unhappiness, unfulfillment and discontentment with our lives. We compare poorly and incorrectly, which is the main issue.We are our own worst critics and tend to point out our own shortcomings first. Comparing ourselves to others highlights our weaknesses while dismissing theirs.

Comparisons are unjust in general. Comparing yourself to others wastes energy because it directs attention away from the adjustments you may be doing to lessen the temptation to compare and toward someone whose life you cannot control. Comparing ourselves to others is fuelled by a sense of self-deficit, low self-esteem, or envy of someone who possesses what we desire. In the end, the comparison doesn't help us get better, get what we want, or get better at what we feel is lacking.When you try to judge someone only by what you see, all other aspects are excluded from the picture, including the imperfect and negative parts.This results in an infinite series of comparisons, none of which you can win because they keep generating new ones. Therefore, we must turn our attention back to ourselves in order to reduce the tendency to compare. Focus on what makes us extraordinary. We can achieve this goal by making simple psychological changes that boost self-esteem and inspire positive change. Pay attention to the things that make you feel awake and alive, and then feed them.

Giving

Giving has been proven to boost your mood and make you feel more in control of your own life. Show kindness, be helpful, and do charity. These little moments of empathy will help others, boost your brain, and benefit your own well-being.

Sharpening Interpersonal Skills

There are so many ways to learn, and it doesn't have to be difficult or intimidating. Just think about what you want to gain and go for it! The influence of others who are healthily inclined towards goodness is often an inspiration. Power is a person's ability to work with others and their own self- efficacy. They set the bar high. They're motivating. They promote a good worldview among their peers. They are ambitious but stable, assertive but courteous, and successful but modest. Someone who is trustworthy, confident, and well-organised is likely to be given more respect in professional areas. These represent examples of personal power in action. Strong interpersonal skills define a person.

Practising Gratitude

I would often do these two things to practise gratitude: first, work on my connection with God. When I work on strengthening my bond with my creator, it gives me a sense of knowing that I am enough and Allah (s.w.t.) alone is enough. When we come to the realisation that this whole universe is governed by a Creator and all of our affairs are arranged according to His plan, what is left to worry about? If we really embed this way of thinking deep inside of us, *inshāʾAllāh*, we will be led to a broadened horizon in acknowledging the true art of gratitude. *Shukr* in Islam is believing that Allah (s.w.t.) has a great plan in terms of each and every one of our *rizq* and provision. It is also said that if we are thankful for what is given and practice sincerity in accepting what has been provided for us in life.

Sharing Stories is Fulfilling

In the future, when you have control of life itself, you can tell stories on how you survived and share them with the people in need of a survival guide that they can refer to as a manual for them to navigate life's rough storms.Write your story and survival guide. Life itself has a funny and magical way where it can drive us to the top and down. Life itself served us pain and also gain. Life gives us treacherous roads that lead to pearls of wisdom. Life gives us the things we need to grow and thrive. If we never learned about pain, if we never learned to feel difficulty, if we never learned to feel anxiety, if we never felt anger, if we never felt hopeless, if we never felt empty, if we never felt all the things that we don't want to feel that give us discomfort, I bet we will never evolve and know the secret of survival and facing the obstacles and fears in life.We need to allow ourselves to feel all the emotions and feelings in order to gain insights and learn the tricks and tips for navigating life. You need to know that an experience with a good balance and mixture of toughness and sweetness will empower you and lead you to inventing your own survival guide.You can write about how you survived the storm and how you mightily and courageously slayed the dragons along the way to reach your kingdom. I bet it would be such an adventurous journey and endeavour. Share your survival kit and story with the world; the people in intense confusion, anxiety, depression, and difficulty would be most in need of them. Believe me.I had been a survival guide seeker from the stories of people that instil hope and faith in me and I could say without the mercy of Allah (s.w.t.) to guide me in revealing these stories I would probably never know how to breathe again. Hence thank you very much to the storytellers and survival kit inventors. You are a true hero.

Seeking Companion

Know that in seeking a companion, you are not afraid of being alone and invalidated, but to have a companion is to know that we share the same core values and principles in having each other back in navigating life's journey. Know that in seeking a companion, you are not afraid of being alone and invalidated, but to have a companion is to know that we share the same core values and principles in having each other back in navigating life's journey.

Knowing Your Rights

Human rights are extremely important in Islam. Hurting someone emotionally, physically, or mentally is a serious sin in Allah's (s.w.t.) view, and He alone will deal with it in this life and the Hereafter. Muslims must exercise extreme caution while using language or taking actions that might offend others. I know it won't always be easy to cut yourself off from or remove yourself from toxic people or environments in life, but believe me, it will always be the best thing you can do for your emotional and physical health. For the people who treat people with disrespect and inhumanity, I want you to know that one day your loved ones, family, friends, daughter, son, niece, nephew, sister, brother, or anybody close to you will enter the working world, and would you like to see them receiving the same treatment that you gave to an innocent employer and succumb to low morale? Your wants and needs are important. It is important to know that in life, what you allow, what you disallow, and what you promote teach people how to treat you.We must acknowledge our emotions, stand up for ourselves, realise our feelings, do what we enjoy, and take time for ourselves.Honour and respect are rights that Islam upholds; as such, it is forbidden for anyone, believer or not, to make fun of or insult others. Says our beloved Prophet (s.a.w.):

The best among you is the one who doesn't harm others with his tongue and hands.

One should not humiliate and disrespect another human, especially in public. The humanness of all human beings is to be respected and considered an end in itself.

The truth is, we can't control the people and environment around us, but we can choose how to respond and save ourselves. Learn to focus on yourself, get to know your essentials and work on them, and prioritise your stable state of mind by seeking your reason for existence in life.Take care of your whole well-being and avoid prolonged isolation that will result in loneliness, as we are creatures who are built in need of connections. Connection helps give us a sense of belonging. Seek out someone you can trust to listen to your problems and provide you with the support you need. A good support system can be found in a social system such as a friend, a soulmate, a family member, or a community. If you feel too overwhelmed, too anxious, too depressed, feeling lost and confused, and being off balance, go and seek a professional's help and assistance for recovery and therapy. But I would like to advise on finding a good professional based on my own experience, because this is indeed a crucial part of building a picture of what real and true therapy is and also ingraining trust in the therapist itself. A true therapist actually listens attentively and responds to you verbally or nonverbally. You will feel validated. You view them as an ally. A good therapist acts as an ally. From your very first session together, they'll work to forge a bond with you that's based on mutual trust. This is known as a therapeutic alliance. They earn your trust. When you have someone's trust, you feel comfortable and supported and may speak freely without worrying about being judged. After one or two sessions, you should be able to tell whether you trust them, and if not, it might not be worthwhile to continue working with them in order to see if they can win your trust. If your therapist ever makes you feel stupid, damaged, or guilty, it's time to reconsider the relationship. They offer a range of solutions.

There's no one-size-fits-all treatment plan. If a particular intervention doesn't work for you, your therapist should be able to provide other suggestions. They're there to offer you a toolbox instead of a single tool. They're open to alternatives. They don't rush your treatment. Both you and your therapist should be on the same page regarding the goals of your treatment and the estimated timeline for achieving those goals. They're mindful of all aspects of your identity.

In conclusion, the good state of our mental health is a precious gem that we ought to protect and it has to start with us wanting it to happen.

Dear you,

There was a moment when I was tested with great pain. A pain that hurts the heart so badly, wounds the soul so deeply, terrorises the mind tragically, trembles the spirit off balance, aches the body all over the place, sucking the light and hope in me, and drains all the energy in me, leaving me exhausted. It was all true pain. I cried to Allah (s.w.t.).

"YA ALLAH. YA ALLAH. YA ALLAH. IT HURTS. IT HURTS. IT HURTS, YA ALLAH. IT HURTS SO BAD."

I had no du'a' in mind. Words could not come out, the pain I felt was immense and undescribable and I just cried to Allah (s.w.t.) while saying His name with all my heart. And within all that crying, I suddenly felt relieved and felt a little bit lighter. I was surprised that by merely crying to Him, my heart could find ease and relief. It was a miraculous moment that moved me. Without a word I said, He understood. He is indeed the Most Understanding, most loving and most compassionate.

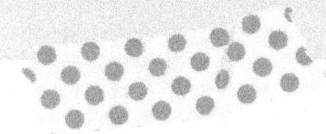

When there are so many troubles in life, when there are so many things we have to face and think of, when there are so many difficult people we have to deal with, and when everything seems disappointing and overwhelming, we put our hope and trust in Allah (s.w.t.) alone. We run to him and cry our hearts out. Allah (s.w.t.) is the only hope when all hope has been lost. Allah (s.w.t.) is the helper when everyone turns away.

Yours truly,

Sharifah Nadirah

I wonder how you find strength in days where you can't understand yourself at length; I wonder how you find hope in days where you don't know how to cope; I wonder how you find feelings that make you warm when you have to face the storm while going against all norms; I wonder how you find yourself to be tamed in going through the fiery flame; I wonder how you let your faith sustain in coexisting with pain; I wonder how you can be kind in days when you find it hard to untangle your messy mind; I wonder how you can smile when life challenges have threw you to miles. I wonder how you remain sane on cloudy days where it never stops to rain. I wonder how you came so far and survived to stay alive, be revived, and magnificently thrive.

EMBRACING SELF-HEALING

As I resumed reading, I started exploring genres about people's life experiences and found that most influential people started with inauthentic lives but then realised they were not making the most of them. Inauthenticity made them feel caged and unable to unleash their fullest potential. Eventually, they broke free, seizing every opportunity while unravelling their genuine core potential and making a change in the world. These stories inspired me, and I aspire to be like them and embrace the traveller in me.

As I reflected on these stories, I began to write about workable ways for me to achieve my authenticity in my journal. The basic rule was to be present, mindful, and bring my focus to the present. The same principle applies when dealing with pain. Pain will not resolve when left untreated or unconfronted;

it will be left unhealed and somehow cause you more pain and chaos in your present moment, hindering your true growth.

As humans, we can't just beat ourselves up into accepting and forgiving ourselves or others. Making peace is a challenging journey that requires patience and persistence. The outcome does not happen overnight; it is a process and progress that we need to venture into and go through.

When we have certain images of how we believe life should be and find it difficult to accept when those images do not match reality, it can sometimes become overwhelming. The negative impact can hit us so hard that it affects our ability to perceive reality and embrace rationality and sanity. Filtering out thoughts and actions that no longer benefit you takes time. If you put in the work, you'll soon discover a more sincere alignment with your inner self.

To achieve a good practice of self-care, you have to slow down, reflect on the ideology of real self-care, accept yourself, let go of what does not contribute to your well-being, be present, and express gratitude for the life you are living to God. Most of us do not like to be offered instant solutions without being seen, heard, and understood. In therapy,

I learned to willingly move through a flow of emotions, which includes a series of positive and uncomfortable emotions. My therapist even told me that I might dwell or go in circles while learning about my emotions. Thus, I learned to gradually not be negatively judgemental or dismissive of that experience and to create a space for myself to experience these emotions and process things without rejection and regression.

From there, I allowed myself to recognise the emotions before acknowledging, accepting, expressing, understanding, and embracing them. This is what emotional validation is all about. Emotional validation is one of the important, unseen, and promoted solutions in these books. It suggests and inspires you to be connected with your emotions. From here, you will learn to regulate, manage, and find balance, and start taking sane steps to move forward and advance on actions of growth.

Therefore, self-healing is about taking responsibility for our well-being and actively working towards our own healing. Self-healing doesn't necessarily mean dismissing modern medicine, doctors, psychologists, psychiatrists, counsellors, and also no longer seeking the right support and resources that can aid us in our journey and completely relying on ourselves to heal. It's an additional way suggested by therapists in aiding this recovery journey of ours. By investing in our own healing, we can create a foundation for a more fulfilling and meaningful life and inspiring growth. Growth and healing are associated, as growth cannot happen until we are capable of healing. We can only grow to the level that our healing allows us to.

Accept yourself for the kindness you bring to the people. When you feel ugly and hate yourself, remember that you are beautifully created by Allah (s.w.t.). You are created in your greatest form by Allah (s.w.t.) and honoured by Him. Accept the smiles and laughter you bring to the people you love. Accept the hopes and dreams. Accept every good thing that you have done to a person that far outweighs any flaw you have. By knowing that you can bring goodness to people, it completely changes how you view yourself. Allow yourself to have your own space and time. Don't force yourself to always be OK when you feel overwhelmed. Choose to isolate and contemplate, and when you are emotionally and mentally ready, find someone close and trusted to express your feelings to and work on sorting out your emotions and feelings to be centred and sane again.

Take care of your physical and mental health. Do things that can nourish them both, such as exercising, staying hydrated, maintaining a good diet, avoiding and removing yourself from toxic people and environments to reduce stress, and find a healthy circle that can be your support system.

It's a rewarding and life-changing moment when you choose to shift your focus from negative and toxic people or vibes to working on your strengths, potential, skills, and talent for the sake of your growth to thrive and evolve towards positive transformation, betterment, and goodness. At this age, I learned that interdependence is much more crucial than solely prioritising independence. The fundamental of interdependence is being able to be independent at first. Working towards independence to offer yourself and your soulmate or loved ones interdependence is an empowering and inspirational act. The strongest and most inspiring women are those who accept, cherish, and appreciate their psychological and physical abilities and capabilities given by God. These pioneers can start offering acts of interdependence. They believe that they have their own noble role in shaping the community. They know that women are uniquely endowed by

God with their own unique and graceful attributes that make this world a better place to live.

Don't allow the wrong people to disrespect your boundaries. Don't let them constantly stress and pressure you to manipulate you, use you, and take advantage of you. If they negatively judge, harshly criticise, belittle, and discriminate, that's your cue to leave. Life is too short to invest your time and energy in things that deteriorate your mental health. Don't allow people to define and mould you into something that is not you; you are beautiful the way you are. Don't let anyone tell you that you are undeserving. Protect your authenticity and hold on to your integrity, morality, and identity. Stay true to who you are and be proud of your originality.

Learn to not attach your value to external factors in life. Seeking constant validation and approval from others will only add to the pain. Learn to not always associate your worth with people or anything. For me personally, being a people pleaser can sometimes risk your own authenticity. I was always a people pleaser in the past because I had a dire desire to fit in, to make people like me. But slowly, I felt empty; it was like nothing was left in my cup after I poured all the compliments and praises into other people's cups. I felt empty and felt that I had been slowly sacrificing my originality and identity to make people happy. So, in the end, I stopped. Whoever wants to stay truly appreciates, celebrates, and is warmly welcomed, and to those who choose to leave because of my authenticity, the door is wide open for you to step out.

You don't need to always impress people; you don't need to force yourself to have constant energy to keep entertaining people when you are at your lowest energy level. And don't set your expectations too high. Sometimes, even if you treat a person nicely and they don't reciprocate the same energy, you could withdraw because you're human and you have your limits and tiredness. It's OK to stop or rest from engaging with people who don't share the same wavelength and learn to not overthink or be so hard on yourself. The right ones will stay. You don't need to explain everything that's going on in your life. You don't have to care about the judgements and nasty criticism people throw at you. You don't have to care about why people do not want to contact you, what people will think of you, or tire yourself to please the people around you when you are tired. Let them be; you have cared enough. Now, just take a leave and spend time for yourself. Allow the judgements and underestimation of others to propel you to build kingdoms and empires. Don't let the negative words of others deteriorate you but allow them to make you grow and thrive. Take time to breathe and enjoy life at your own pace. Allow yourself to have a hobby, an interest, or even a passion to explore to keep you focused and closer to self-acceptance and originality. When you have something to do in life, such as a dream to chase, you will remain determined, and thus, self-acceptance comes to embrace your dear self.

Hence, focus on what will make you proud of yourself and work on it. Allow what you love to lead your way. Prioritise what YOU want to be, not what others want you to be. Be firm in your principles. Hold on tight to them. Be confident in your dream and work on climbing the ladder to the top. Keep progressing so you'll know that you're on a path that's leading you to something. Your dream is nothing less than their dreams. STAY FOCUS AND CONFIDENT. Keep unlocking goals and reaching milestones on the path that you choose. Hence, you will one day be highly contributing to interdependency when you acknowledge your authenticity and identity. Choose to grow on your own ground in your own peculiar way and work on ways to always be independent rather than dependent. If you want something to be successful, work on it; don't expect anybody to do it for you. Allow pain and hardship to be the teacher in teaching the meaning and wisdom of life. Allow the hurtful words of others to make you grow and thrive.

Dear you,

Oftentimes, I heard that fulfilling a partner's rights had always been highlighted on the financial or economic aspect, and these aspects are often assumed to be the most reliable way to secure a happy marriage, traditionally and conventionally. But the truth is, Islam has taught a holistic approach to navigating marriage life. Islam has taught us to pay attention to other crucial aspects too. For example, emotional, mental, spiritual, and intellectual aspects are also the needs and obligations that have to be met in taking care of and fulfilling the rights of the family members, as highlighted in the teachings of Islam to build a harmonious family.

The importance of protecting a partner's mental health in navigating marriage life is crucial, which includes eliminating one's toxic traits, negligence, and inattentiveness towards their partner's feelings and emotions. Putting one's ego aside and providing emotional support for the partner should always be incorporated into marriage. The importance of spirituality is to not only possess a wealth of religious knowledge and appear to act or talk about religion, but also to know and understand how the teachings of Islam can be executed and practised for the betterment of marriage. The importance of educating a partner with beneficial knowledge does not stop at religious knowledge; it goes beyond that. This includes encouraging the partner to learn beneficial knowledge, for example, by enrolling in courses related to childhood education, entertaining questions from the partner on a course they took and learned related to 'healthy relationships' without complaint or downgrading them, and not only limiting a wife's capability to cooking or house chores. We can be inspired by how Prophet Muhammad (s.a.w.) educates, protects, and guides 'A'ishah (r.a.) in the holistic aspects that make 'A'ishah (r.a.) grow and bloom in becoming an Islamic scholar where the people have referred her. Masha' Allah, this moved me so much. Prophet Muhammad (s.a.w.) is truly an inspiration.

Thus, when I heard statements such as: "It doesn't matter how he treats me as long as he can support the family financially." "It's OK if he doesn't do anything in the household except work for money." "It's OK if he doesn't care for me and the kids as long as he is rich and wealthy!" "It's OK if he denies my rights to be educated as long as he pays for the bills." I once watched a video of a husband who gave a large amount of monthly pocket money to his wife but treated her poorly, and the wife was OK with that. I became frustrated and disappointed. Hence, I began to question things: Is the financial aspect the only aspect that can really secure the family alone while ignoring other aspects that need to be included and paid attention to?

Is it truly safe for family institutions to only prioritise the financial aspect while neglecting other aspects that need to be incorporated into the household? Does focusing on one aspect of the household keep the family afloat? Or maybe it does work for certain individuals, but never for those who understand the meaning of humanity, embody the teachings of Islam, strongly uphold one's values, and prioritise one's core beliefs. I personally believe it is essential to manage and work on all aspects holistically in navigating marriage life, as it is aligned with human needs and Islamic teachings. It shows respect for human values.

I truly believe that a couple who chooses a holistic approach to navigating married life should not only focus on the financial aspect but also consider other critical factors such as the emotional, mental, physical, spiritual, and intellectual aspects. Often, we conventionally believe that a partner's responsibility is solely to be financially sufficient, overlooking the other vital factors that keep a marriage functional. These include effective and transparent communication, getting to know each other without barriers or walls, discussing things openly and professionally, being emotionally present, supporting each other's passions and dreams, showing understanding and appreciation, and educating each other.

Marriage, to me, is more than just wealth; it also considers human resources. For example, prioritising the human touch demonstrates awareness of the safety and importance of mental and emotional health, which can impact the entire household. How can one extend empathy and compassion during difficult times? Poor treatment and neglect in these areas can lead to unseen problems and harm the marriage institution. Having a spouse who encourages you to learn healthy parenting styles, end generational trauma, raise mentally healthy children, educate yourself on mental well-being, find your calling, and be a good role model is crucial.

With knowledge comes wisdom to navigate marriage and life itself. Giving wealth to someone lacking knowledge may result in the wealth being squandered overnight. Whenever I hear that money and wealth are above all aspects and are eroding human values in marriage, I beg to differ. I believe in protecting one's values, beliefs, dignity, and principles. I absolutely disagree with allowing any immoral or unethical behaviour in marriage in the name of wealth, fame, or position that degrades one's worth as a human.

Money and wealth can never buy genuine love, original personalities, authenticity, integrity, or morality. What governs wealth is knowledge and human values. Money should be a tool that enables us to build relationships, not an ego booster that places us above others. People with money have the power to reduce our self-worth if we allow it. Money should not be above humanity or rob us of our human values in marriage. Cooperation is necessary, and anyone's rights or roles should not be silenced by money.

Therefore, anyone who believes that money is the only solution to making a partner happy should know that there are many aspects to discover and educate themselves on to ensure the longevity of a marriage. Be wise and choose what makes you more valuable and human.

Yours sincerely,

Sharifah Nadirah

When individuals in positions of authority introduce endless terminology to forcefully impose a new ideology on society, they are donning a false 'educated mentality' and guilt-tripping people into accepting inferiority. This process disconnects individuals from their true selves, gaslights the community into thinking illogically, denies human nature, and detaches individuals from their origins, all while leading mankind towards confusion and bewilderment.

FAILURE, CHALLENGES, HOPE AND SUCCESS

We are often taught that failure signifies the end of hope and success. When things go wrong, we feel devastated. However, failure isn't as dreadful as it seems. It is simply a lack of success or the absence of a desired or expected outcome, indicating that our expectations were not met. Failure is a learning experience that everyone must undergo. As humans, we naturally grapple with hardships and failures in life, despite knowing that they are inevitable. Dealing with failure can always be challenging.

A Journey of Failure

Failure is not a word that is only solely used when it comes to flunking in school, college, universities or even at work but the word failure itself can be used to indicate many unsuccessful things in life ever since we are in our childhood days to the world of an adult.

Personally, I have experienced numerous failures. As a child, I failed to listen to my parents and often behaved rebelliously. I failed to find true friends in primary school due to the prevalence of cliques. In secondary school, I failed to excel in mathematics and protect myself from bullying. These failures continued into adulthood, where I struggled with my mental health, leading to anxiety disorders.

My journey with failure has been difficult, but it has also taught me valuable lessons. Failure has made me more empathetic and kind, as I understand the importance of treating others with compassion. Despite the challenges, I believe that one day, I will rise again from this fall and be welcomed by the light.

I've experienced many failures in life, and to be honest, I've failed in numerous aspects. As a child, I failed to listen to my parents and became a rebel. I couldn't stop myself from climbing onto my house's roof to avoid my mother while I hadn't yet finished my homework, just to call out to my neighbour to play. In primary school, I failed to find true friends, as most students stuck to their cliques. I vividly remember the school culture, where everyone categorised themselves into groups, including the prefects, who mostly mingled only with other prefects in their cliques. I recall one librarian prefect who threw a private birthday party at school during recess, exclusively for prefects. When we tried to take a peek, we were chased away. In primary school, I also struggled in mathematics and was frequently scolded by the maths teacher, which made me scared to try and learn. Additionally, I failed to protect myself from bullying. There was a boy in my class who would shout, throw things, and bang on desks to intimidate me, partly because I would always talk back to stand up for myself.

As a junior secondary school student, I failed to fit society's standards of beauty and was called ugly to my face by a senior. I also failed to trust the right people, which led to my secrets becoming rumours. I failed to find friends who wouldn't backbite and call me names. There was a duo of girls who were known for saying nasty things about people and cursing a lot, and I was one of their victims. I remember being with a group of friends who would backbite and speak ill of each other, with the leader being a school prefect who decided who could stay in the group. There was a girl in the group who was also a prefect and would often get into trouble with the leader. The leader disliked this girl because she was honest and would express disagreement, unlike others who would blindly obey. When the leader tried to kick the girl out of the group, I refused to follow the rules because the girl didn't deserve such treatment. As a result, I was the next candidate to be evicted from the group. This incident occurred when I was selected to represent the school for an international program. One day, I approached the group leader to discuss the dress code for the program, seeking her opinion. Instead, she became mad and told me I was not qualified to be selected. After the incident, I was no longer in the group. As a senior secondary school student, I failed in my science subjects.

In college or university, I failed the final clinical examination for the second time. I vividly remember crying during the eye examination after learning of my failure. I was completely burned out, and the lecturer scolded me for crying during the examination, saying she had no time for drama. During my final year as a university student, I faced many burnouts. I remember a particularly painful experience during my final clinical exam, where I was told by the supervisor in front of a patient that my steps were wrong. I believed my steps were correct because I had studied them thoroughly, but I lacked the confidence to assert myself. After the exam, the supervisor criticised me harshly, making me feel worthless. The next day, I sought the opinion of another supervisor, who confirmed that my steps were correct. Despite this, I never received justice for the way I was treated by the initial supervisor. However, this experience taught me that kindness exists and inspired me to be more empathetic and kind to others.

Failure continued to impact my life as I entered adulthood and began experiencing episodes of anxiety disorders. This was a dark period in my life, as I felt like I had failed in every aspect of life. I felt useless and was thrown into a deep abyss of darkness. I failed to meet expectations in my roles as a servant of Allah, a wife, a daughter, a sister, a friend, an employee, and a student. These failures were rooted in my struggles with mental health. Despite my challenges, I am grateful for the few loved ones and friends who supported me during these difficult times. They showed me that goodness exists, and I strive to be kind and empathetic to others, as we never know what someone else is going through.

I was desperately hoping for a light to lead me out of all this misery. I truly wanted to rise again and rewrite my story. But my health at that moment didn't allow it. I always preferred to stay in my room and avoid people. Talking to others drained my energy and triggered my anxiety, so I craved solitude. This was my coping mechanism, my way of unwinding. However, this preference for solitude led to misunderstandings among people. They thought I purposely chose not to socialise and isolate myself. They saw me as the weird one always alone in my room. If only they knew how much I wanted to avoid troubling anyone by staying in my room, how much I just wanted to hide and avoid causing further trouble.

At my lowest point, I became emotionally oversensitive, and this perception of me as fragile and overly emotional became an issue. People couldn't understand that I just wanted to be understood, not judged. There came a moment when I had to resign from work and take a break from my studies.

Some saw me as jobless, useless, and a non-contributor. It was disheartening to be viewed as weak and a failure, especially after enduring so much and reaching a breaking point of severe depression and anxiety disorder. I felt like I had blown up from life.

During this period, even a friend commented that I was different from the cheerful and outgoing person I used to be. Honestly, my mind was so overwhelmed that I didn't even realise the changes in my character or behaviour. Thankfully, I had a few loved ones and close friends who became my support system. They understood, cared, and stayed by my side. *alḥamdulillāh*.

In that moment, as much as I wanted to give up and succumb to darkness, I also desperately wanted to regain my health and rise again. Despite believing that I would remain in darkness forever, I also held onto the hope that one day, I would rise again and be welcomed by the light.

The Light that Shines From Passion

After years of struggling and battling, I found the energy and time to do what I love. There were many lessons learned from past failures that contributed to my growth and current success. While I once hated my failures intensely, that hatred eventually wore me out to a point where I began to shift my mindset. I started to believe that there might be valuable messages behind these episodes of failure, perhaps even miracles or wisdom guiding me to a better path. Failure became the fuel that drove me toward success, challenging me to prove to myself that I could make things happen.

You can't ignore the negative emotions that come with failure. However, it's these emotions that often lead to better performance next time. A recent study published in the *Journal of Psychology of Sport and Exercise*, titled *Is failing the key to success? : A randomised experiment investigating goal attainment effects on cognitions, emotions, and subsequent performance* suggests that failures can impact self-esteem but have little effect on performance. This contradicts the common belief that failure breeds more failure.

Negative feelings after failing are a crucial part of the process. The key is to avoid being consumed by negativity and focus on using those feelings as fuel. What I learned from failure is that your attitude towards it and how you react to it are crucial. It's about using failure as an opportunity to succeed rather than seeing it as a defeat. It's about seeing failure not as a barrier but as a chance to move forward and be better.

According to psychologists Daniel Kahneman and Amos Tversky, winners are more fearful of losing than losers are eager to win. Their research showed that the impact of a defeat is twice as great as the benefit of a victory, highlighting the significant negative impact that failure can have on us.

People of Success Who Have Failed

The truth is, most people hate to fail. The word 'failure' itself instils fear in us. Many people are afraid of failing, and it seems like everyone wants success immediately. Many of us prefer the fast track to success, aiming to be successful instantly without being judged by our failures along the way. We aspire to perfection and to be the very best in life, seeking approval, celebration, and appreciation. We don't want to be looked down upon. Failing is indeed a lonely and uncomfortable feeling, to not be welcomed or valued. I can relate and understand. It's painful. But I want you to know that encountering failure is not always a terrible thing. Instead, it merely serves as evidence that success does not come easily. It takes time and effort to succeed. In reality, before you succeed in life, you may experience numerous failures. The route taken to get there, rather than the final destination, often defines a person. The story of our process and progress is what is needed to inspire people and be their guide throughout their journey towards success. At the end of the day, people are more interested in how you overcome obstacles and persist toward your goals. Your story of overcoming failures will empower those who are in need of light. Hence, the way failure is perceived needs to change. Failure is an opportunity to learn something that is flawed! It is an opportunity to grow and learn. Success is born out of failure. Anyone who has attempted to make their life worthwhile has failed. This is precisely the reason you need to change your attitude toward it. When you eventually realise that failure is the catalyst for achievement, you may begin to realise your full potential.

Honestly, the world is full of people who have succeeded in failing. Any successful person will tell you that they have failed at some point along the way. You'll probably hear a lot of tales about errors and mistakes. To succeed, many of them overcame obstacles like doubters, failures, and career setbacks. They were determined, and like an old-fashioned alchemist, they transformed their metal into gold. Some of the most successful people in the world had epic failures prior to their success. We applaud their accomplishments but frequently forget the journey that brought them there, a route that is frequently fraught with failure. Instead, it only shows that success is not something that comes easily. To achieve, you must put in time and effort. In actuality, you might go through a lot of failures in life before you achieve.

Here is one of the inspiring successful figures who I look up to, who had once gone through a period of downfalls. But she recovered and was ultimately successful. Let's now go through the challenges that she encountered.

Puan Anita Abu Bakar

Puan Anita Abu Bakar is the Founder and President of the Mental Illness Awareness & Support Association (MIASA). Her story of battling mental illness has given a spark of hope and faith to those who are also struggling and fighting with mental disorders. She reunites people and gives them friends to share feelings, emotions, and problems with, as they share the same story of surviving mental illness. It is a lonely and scary feeling to go through the battle alone without a strong support system. It's really doubtful and fearful to walk alone and not have people to instil within you the confidence that you will get through this and survive (and one day you will eventually thrive) while facing stigma. Hence, the establishment of MIASA caters to all of these concerns, providing and offering mental health services to cater to people's needs. This is indeed a noble act, as she knew how painful and cold it was to walk alone. She created MIASA so that people out there would feel less lonely.

> *The conceptualisation and birth of MIASA, the Mental Illness Awareness & Support Association, happened in 2017 due to the realisation of the many gaps that exist in the mental health system and how many continue to be silenced by stigma and discrimination daily. With hopes and aspirations to work for change, I formed MIASA, with the support of my husband, my family, friends, and many unsung heroes. MIASA is a Mental Health Advocacy and Peer Support group based in Selangor, formed and run by peers for peers, the very first of its kind in Malaysia. The hope is that via this platform, people would have a place to go, a safe space for them to get help, be supported, and empowered in their journey to recovery.*
>
> (Puan Anita)

I learned from Puan Anita's story that she started having episodes of panic attacks when she was working in the United States because of all the stress and trauma she was going through at the time. Upon returning to Malaysia, she was shouldering the responsibility of raising her two young children while working and pursuing her MBA. All of this demanded a lot from her, especially in terms of time and energy, which had an adverse effect on her. Moreover, due to her eagerness in chasing success and meeting KPIs, she became overworked and neglected to care for herself. Eventually, due to a lack of sleep, rest, and attention to her needs, her body and brain gave out. She went through severe panic attacks until it was sometimes impossible for her to breathe. It was too much for her and she crumbled. She ceased functioning in life. She lost the ability to care for her husband and children. She lost the ability to drive, work, and interact with others, and developed a fear of everything. She felt extremely lost. She was unable to comprehend it and was unsure of what to do. She felt disconnected, alone, emptied, and trapped as she sunk into a deep, black pit. When she was initially diagnosed, she didn't know what she was going through, had no idea where to turn for assistance, and didn't know anyone who had the disease to share things with.

She never knew that without proper care, support, and therapy, mental health issues might seriously impair one's ability to function. At that moment, she felt very defeated. After everything she had achieved in life, after the success she gained, here she was, feeling crippled by her own anxiety, fear, and panic. She felt so ashamed of her state and like a burden to everyone for not being able to function. She pushed everyone away, especially her kids. Every day seemed like a long, agonising death for her.

Until one day, she was engaged with the thought of people who took their own lives in an effort to soothe themselves and feel like their suffering would soon be over. She was astounded that she could relate to this and rushed to pray right away. She confessed to God her ignorance of His purposes. And in this way, for the first time in her entire life, she submitted herself fully to God (which was the most beautiful part of her story). Then she drew everyone back up to her. In the end, she stopped doubting and complaining about her condition and overcame difficulties with the help and support of her family.

Having a mental health disorder is the hardest thing that I have ever experienced in my 30-plus years of living hands down, but crossing over to recovery was even harder. Through my many rock bottoms and experience in this journey to finally finding my willpower and strength through surrendering totally to Allah (s.w.t.) and seeking knowledge, getting treatment and support, I finally could stand on my own two feet again alḥamdulillāh. I finally understood the lessons that I had to learn and that without HIM, I was nothing and that I was completely at HIS mercy.

Now, apart from Puan Anita Abu Bakar being the Founder and President of the Mental Illness Awareness & Support Association (MIASA), she also initiated the first Peer-led Mental Health Advocacy and Support Group in Malaysia. She established 'The Orchid Clubhouse', Malaysia's first Mental Health Crisis management. Puan Anita also initiated the National Advocacy for Mental Health Association (NAMhA) in 2021 and was appointed as the Chairperson for NAMH, the first peer-based mental health alliance in Malaysia. Puan Anita is also the Founder and Managing Director of Qaiser Darussalam Publications. She is also very involved in educating the public and making herself & peers heard via her participation as a guest speaker and panellist in many conferences and programs nationally and internationally and was the first Mental Health group to ever present in Parliament on mental health, its gaps and solutions moving forward.

Moreover, Puan Anita was the official selected winner of the Patient Champion for Science and Medicine award by the International Metrodora Awards. She owns programs under MIASA named *Journey to Recovery* and *Kembara Syifa*, which have aired on IKIM.FM, a local Islamic radio station. She has also been interviewed by ABC News Australia and Islamic Channel UK and was recently on the ListenWell Podcast by Viatris, alongside Dr. Javed, the President of the World Psychiatric Association. She is also a member of the Advisory Board, the International Federation of Pharmaceutical Manufacturers and Association (IFPMA). This year, Puan Anita was appointed as a member council of the Mental Health Promotion and Advisory Council under MOH.

Failure in the Islamic Perspective

Usually, because of the difficulties we face, we often think that Allah (s.w.t.) does not want joy, happiness, and success for us. We may believe that we are not meant to be winners or that we do not deserve victory, succumbing to the belief that Allah (s.w.t.) does not love us. However, the truth is that the tests, including the difficult times that people go through, are a part of the laws of Allah (s.w.t.) that govern this universe. They are not always something bad; instead, they are a challenge we face that could be a test of our patience and endurance, a lesson, a reminder, a way to purify ourselves from sins and errors, or all of these things at once.

When something does not work for us, it is a way of Allah (s.w.t.) redirecting us to a better path, telling us to wait, or saving us from a harmful unknown danger. It is also a way for Allah (s.w.t.) to teach us human values and noble characteristics. The truth is that nothing is an absolute failure; there is always a gain and an advantage in our challenging hardships. A hardship indicates Allah's (s.w.t.) mercy. Allah (s.w.t.) tests us with failures and hardships, but at the same time, He also promises to give us ease. In the Qur'an, Allah (s.w.t.) tells us that we will experience hardship, but He also promises us twice the ease:

For indeed, with hardship [will be] ease [i.e., relief]. Indeed, with hardship [will be] ease.

(*surah* al-Inshirah, 94:5-6).

In His boundless generosity, Allah (s.w.t.) has made it crystal clear that although we will experience hardships, setbacks, and difficult times, ease will always come double. In these verses, we can see that Allah (s.w.t.)wants us to change the way we view difficulties and potential failures in our lives. The verses above are from *surah* al-Inshirah. The *surah* comforts, consoles, and provides solace to the souls of the believers. The *surah* was revealed in Makkah in the early days of Islam, which was a time of extreme struggle for the Muslims due to the continued opposition toward the Islamic message and Prophet Muhammad (s.a.w.). *Surah* al-Inshirah was sent to the Prophet (s.a.w.) and his *ummah* as a word of encouragement from Allah (s.w.t.).

Although the lives of the Prophets aren't normally associated with the word failure, they did face many challenges throughout their lives. Every single one of them went through struggles related to perceived failures, but due to their way of thinking and the faith they had in Allah (s.w.t.), they all pulled through and achieved the ultimate triumph. Of all the stories of the prophets, I would like to focus on Prophet Muhammad's story. The Prophet (s.a.w.) undoubtedly experienced many struggles and setbacks on a personal and community level during the course of his whole life in his journey of spreading the message of peace. His story is a beautiful and inspiring one filled with challenges and success, containing a series of victories. He (s.a.w.) was very successful but had gone through the most difficult times in life before achieving a positive outcome. Eventually, he (s.a.w.) was able to overcome all obstacles and emerged from trying times stronger than ever, all because of Allah's (s.w.t.) will and guidance. No one else can serve as a better example of how to handle trials, tribulations, hardships, and challenging situations than our beloved Prophet Muhammad (s.a.w.). He (s.a.w.) was not only a remarkable person with a noble character but was also guided by the revelations from Allah Almighty. In His Infinite mercy, Allah (s.w.t.) has bestowed upon us a gift which is the Prophet (s.a.w.) as a role model so that we can connect with him on many levels and different aspects of life. We can relate to the Prophet (s.a.w.) more deeply as we read through his biography and see the numerous challenges he (s.a.w.) faced. He (s.a.w.) had human limitations; he (s.a.w.) would bleed when experiencing physical injuries and would experience emotional suffering in tested moments, but he (s.a.w.) persisted in his efforts to please Allah (s.w.t.) and reach Paradise despite this. By following the lead of our Beloved Prophet (saw), we can see how he (s.a.w.) adapted to each and every one of the challenging circumstances in which he was placed. Rasulullah (s.a.w.) was the best leader, husband, father, grandfather, and friend.

GLOSSARY

1. *Akhlak:* Morals or manners, often referring to good character.

2. *Alḥamdulillāh ʿalā kulli ḥāl:* "Praise be to Allah in every circumstance." It is a phrase Muslims use to express gratitude to Allah, especially in difficult situations.

3. *Amanah:* Trustworthiness or responsibility.

4. *Awrah:* The parts of the body that should be covered in public according to Islamic teachings.

5. *Ayah:* A verse in the Qurʾan.

6. *Daʿwah:* The act of inviting others to Islam.

7. *Dhikr:* Remembrance of Allah (s.w.t.) in the form of recitation or meditation.

8. *Dunya:* The temporal world, as opposed to the afterlife.

9. *Duʿaʾ:* Supplication or prayer.

10. *Ikhtilat:* Mixing or intermingling of genders in a way that is Islamically prohibited.

11. *Iman:* Faith or belief, especially in the context of Islamic belief in Allah and His Messenger.

12. *Jahannam:* Hellfire, the place of punishment in the afterlife for those who reject Allah's guidance.

13. *Muadhdhin:* The person who calls the adhan (call to prayer).

14. *Naqib/naqibah:* A male/female leader or supervisor, often used in the context of Islamic groups or gatherings.

15. *Niyyah:* Intention, particularly the intention one has when performing an act of worship in Islam.

16. *Rizq:* Provision or sustenance, often used to refer to the sustenance provided by Allah.

17. *Ṣalah:* The Islamic prayers performed five times a day.

18. *Shayṭan:* The devil or Satan, the ultimate source of evil in Islamic belief.

19. *Shukr:* Gratitude or thankfulness.

20. *Surah:* A chapter in the Qur'an.

21. *Ukhuwah fillāh lilāhi taʿala:* Brotherhood/sisterhood for the sake of Allah.

22. *Ummah:* The Muslim community.

23. *Usrah:* A small Islamic study or support group.

24. *Ustadh/ustadha:* Male/female teacher.

25. *ʿAqidah:* Belief or creed, often referring to the core tenets of Islamic belief.

26. *ʿIbadah:* Worship or acts of worship in Islam.

REFERENCES

al-Ghazzālī, Iḥyā' 'Ulūm Al-Dīn, 1:337.

American Art Association website. Accessed December 20, 2016.

American Art Therapy Association. Masters Education Standards. June 30, 2007.

Hanh, Thich Nhat. Reconciliation: Healing the Inner Child. Berkeley, CA: Parallax Press, 2006.

Novotney, Amy. "Awakening the Inner Child." American Psychological Association. Vol. 42, no. 1 (2011): 34.

Sjöblom, M., K. Ohrling, and C. Kostenius. "Useful life lessons for health and well-being: adults' reflections of childhood experiences illuminate the phenomenon of the inner child." International Journal of Qualitative Studies on Health and Well-Being. Vol. 13, issue 1 (2018): 1–9.

Slayton, Susan C., J. D'Archer, and F. Kaplan. "Outcome studies on the efficacy of art therapy: a review of findings." Art Therapy: Journal of the American Art Therapy Association. 27, no. 3 (2011): 108-118.

Vallerand, Robert J. "The role of passion in sustainable psychological well-being." Psych Well-Being 2, no. 1 (2012). https://doi.org/10.1186/2211-1522-2-1.

"Mindfulness." Oxford English Dictionary. https://en.oxforddictionaries.com/definition/mindfulness.

www.ingramcontent.com/pod-product-compliance
Lightning Source LLC
LaVergne TN
LVHW061609070526
838199LV00078B/7223